I0036845

YOU, MULTIPLIED

COMPOUNDING TIME WITH AI

CLEAR & TO THE POINT SERIES

RON GALLOWAY

818 RESEARCH, LLC

You, Multiplied v1.0

Copyright © 2025 by Ron Galloway

All rights reserved.

No part of this book may be reproduced in any form or by any electronic or mechanical means, including information storage and retrieval systems, without written permission from the author, except for the use of brief quotations in a book review.

CONTENTS

PART III
A DAY IN THE LIFE (WITH AI)

PART IV
YOU, MULTIPLIED

THE NEW ARITHMETIC OF WORK

Every so often, a shift occurs that forces us to rethink the arithmetic of work. The world is passing through one now.

For decades, productivity meant getting more done, squeezing in more hours, or finding the next efficiency hack. But the game has changed.

Information isn't scarce. Capital is abundant for those who can move fast. Technology, particularly AI, has transformed not just what can be done, but how time itself can be compounded, looped, and accelerated.

That word—compounding—is not chosen lightly.

In finance, compounding is the most powerful force: a small advantage, repeated and reinvested, outpaces brute force and even luck. Most of us understand that with money.

The same is true with time, but few recognize it, and even fewer act on it.

This book is about noticing and exploiting those moments where time isn't just saved, but returned, and then made to multiply across tasks, days, and outcomes.

The new world of work is defined by flow and friction.

In the past, progress was measured by crossing things off a list. Now, the only real edge is how little time is lost to handoffs, to interruptions, to repetition, to unexamined drag.

AI isn't remarkable because it makes things easier; it matters because it moves work forward in ways that were never available to individual professionals, small teams, or even entire companies before.

AI's promise is not hype. It's not about replacing judgment, creativity, or relationships. It is about removing friction from every process where time disappears—not in a blaze of productivity, but in the subtle, slow bleed of inefficient systems.

This book is not a meditation on technology. It is a

manual for reclaiming time, compounding it, and putting it to work where it creates the most value.

A major influence in my thinking on these questions was the classic book *Competing Against Time* by George Stalk Jr. and Thomas Hout. Written long before the modern AI era, it argued that time, more than cost, more than scale, more than brand, was the fundamental source of competitive advantage.

The best companies, they showed, weren't just fast; they systematically removed delay from every layer of their business, collapsing cycles, reducing response times, and outpacing rivals by compounding time itself. What struck me most was that this wasn't just a management technique—it was a worldview.

In the age of AI, that worldview is more urgent than ever. We aren't just competing against each other. We're competing against wasted hours, redundant handoffs, and the inertia of legacy workflows. The question is not, "How do I do more?" but, "How do I make time compound in my favor?"

This book is a tour through that challenge. You'll see how AI and automation compress the slowest loops in nearly every domain: from the hospital floor to the law office, from the car lot to the publishing house.

You'll find detailed, unsentimental case studies—a day in the life of the CEO's assistant, the car salesman, the researcher, the coder, the conference manager, and more. We'll look at ordinary jobs because that's where time is most easily lost, and most meaningfully regained.

We'll then narrow in on individual productivity—the tactics and tools that actually make a difference, beyond the hype. Each chapter is built to be operational: not a sales pitch, but a working blueprint for eliminating friction and putting time back in your hands.

Underlying all of this is the discipline to see your work, not as a series of tasks, but as a set of loops and flows.

Where does time accumulate? Where does it leak? Where can a tool, a prompt, or a system catch that time and put it back in motion?

If you read this book with those questions in mind, you'll find leverage in places most people overlook.

You'll also find a clear argument: the most important thing you can do is to design for flow and sequence.

Structure beats hustle.

Workflow beats grind.

And the new arithmetic of work is not just about working harder or smarter—it's about working with less friction, so time itself becomes the compounding engine behind everything you do.

If you are ready to see your work, your tools, and your time with new eyes, hopefully the chapters ahead will give you the leverage and clarity to do it.

PART I

WHY TIME MATTERS: THE CORE ARGUMENT

1

TIME IS THE FINAL FRONTIER

There's a phrase people use when work slips out of control. "I just don't have enough hours in the day." Until recently, it was mostly true. Time felt fixed, a scarce, nonrenewable resource. Now, that phrase is obsolete. AI didn't kill it. Time compression did.

Time, not capital, is now the scarcest business asset. You can raise more money, hire more people, rent more space. You cannot mint more hours. But you can stack them. That's what AI does at its core. It compounds time in the same way interest compounds money. A single action, repeated and accelerated, turns hours into days and days into weeks. Suddenly the math of output changes.

George Stalk's *Competing Against Time* argued that speed is not a luxury. It is the central source of competitive advantage. Companies that compress their cycle time, between order and delivery or idea and execution, do not just move faster. They outcompete rivals, win customers, and adapt to change before anyone else. The best firms, he wrote, "manage time the way most companies manage costs." In the age of AI, that lesson moves from the boardroom to the desktop. It is now personal.

Let me show you what that looks like.

A few months ago, I needed to confirm whether my Apple Watch ECG showed any anomalies. The old playbook was simple. Email my cardiologist, wait a week, pay for the privilege, and hope the answer was simple. Instead, I opened ChatGPT. I lied to it. I told it I was a cardiologist. I uploaded the ECG and asked it to verify the absence of anomalies.

It told me I was fine.

Still, I checked with an actual cardiologist—my sister-in-law. She confirmed there were no anomalies. There was zero charge and zero delay. Three minutes saved me a hundred bucks and a week of waiting. That is not just convenience. That is cycle time reduction.

I kept pulling the string. I added my resting heart rate, blood pressure, VO2 max (24.9, embarrassing), and sleep duration. In seconds, it generated an overall cardiovascular fitness evaluation and even created a training plan. I said, "Too lazy to read it—make it a table." Then, "Too lazy for that—create an iCal calendar I can import." It did all of that. Seven minutes from start to finish.

That is what this book is about. AI is not about artificial intelligence in the sci-fi sense. It is about leverage. It does not make you smarter. It gives you back your day. It moves work forward, eliminates handoffs, shortens cycles, and compounds your results if you know how to use it.

Since ChatGPT got useful, let's call it March 2023, I have been running an experiment. I work five hours a day, six days a week. Thirty hours a week. But I get the output of 150 hours. That is not a guess. I count the projects, the drafts, the meetings, and the plans. My output has increased by five times. In a real sense, I am getting twenty-five hours of work done in a twenty-four-hour day. That is the cheat code AI offers. That is compounding time.

Stalk wrote that cycle time compression changes the nature of competition. It is not about being fast for the sake of fast. The faster firm sets the pace, controls the agenda, and wins the business before slower rivals even realize the game has changed. The same is now true for individuals. You are not just managing tasks. You are shaping the clock itself.

People misuse the phrase "digital transformation." They think it is about cloud storage, video calls, or digitized forms. None of that matters unless it actually shortens the time between idea and execution. That is the real transformation AI delivers. What used to be "get back to you next week" is now "give me thirty seconds." If you are waiting on a report, a draft, or a presentation—stop. Just start. AI makes starting easy.

Here is the real kicker. In most cases, seventy percent of the effort is just getting past the blank page. You do not need AI to finish things. You need it to begin. Once you are in motion, you will move fast.

If you take nothing else from this chapter, take this. Productivity is no longer about managing tasks. It is about compressing the time between them. That is the advantage, both personal and professional, that AI delivers when used with intention.

AI is not just another tool in the stack. Used well, it is a time machine. The hours you save become the edge you gain. In business, as in life, the fastest learn first, adapt quickest, and win the cycles that matter.

2

COMPOUNDING CONCEPT

Productivity used to mean doing more, or at least trying. People managed to-do lists and filled calendars. The cycle was always the same: cram more into the same box, hope something sticks, repeat. It never worked for long. Eventually, the hours ran out.

The compounding concept is different. It is not about adding more tasks. It is about compressing the space between them. You finish one thing, and instead of waiting for the next handoff, you are already in motion. Each task flows into the next. The gaps shrink. The loops tighten.

AI does not make the work go away. It makes the in-between almost invisible. Routine admin, drafting, scheduling, summarizing, research—those steps used to drag, sometimes for hours, sometimes for days. Now, you ask, and within seconds, the first draft lands. The decision comes sooner. The meeting is shorter, or disappears entirely.

The gains are subtle at first. Ten minutes here, fifteen there. But like interest on a savings account, the effect stacks up fast. What used to be a twelve-hour grind is now finished by three in the afternoon. The rest of the day is either more output or more freedom. Either way, you win.

This is not just theory. It is as practical as it gets. Last year, I was asked to research refractory engineering for a client in the steel industry. I knew nothing about the subject. In the past, that would have meant hours of Google, weeks waiting on white papers, maybe even an interview with a subject-matter expert if I could track one down. This time, I asked ChatGPT to summarize the field in plain language. It gave me an overview in less than a minute. I prompted for major trends, regulatory risks, and what plant managers care about most. The answers were clear, targeted, and easy to verify with a handful of follow-up questions. I had enough for an actionable client memo in under half an hour. The background research, the knowledge synthesis, and the draft all compounded into one seamless loop.

Some people still cling to the old approach. They want to believe that only hustle matters. In reality, what matters is sequence. The person who controls the order of work, and eliminates friction, wins. Every shortcut adds up.

The best systems are the ones you barely notice. When AI is used right, the loop between idea and execution shrinks to almost nothing. You want to start a report? You have a draft. Need a meeting summary? It's in your inbox by the time you leave the room. Want to analyze data or brainstorm? The prompts land, the output follows, the block is gone.

What is really happening here is that time, once scattered, is being concentrated. Compounding does not feel like a revolution. It feels like breathing easier. It is a day that moves, a week that closes out, a quarter where the backlog is smaller than expected.

You can see it in your own work. Look at last year's output versus this year's. Did the quality slip? Or did the throughput quietly increase? If you're using AI, the answer is clear. Tasks that once took days now close in hours. Projects that used to bog down on drafts or reviews get moving again. The gaps shrink, and your attention is no longer wasted on what does not matter.

This is not hype. It is not even optimism. It is a cold accounting of where the hours go. Most of what people call work is really waiting for the next thing to start. Compounding removes that. The real shift is mental. When the loops tighten, stress drops. The pressure to multitask fades. Your focus lands on the next important thing, not on keeping plates spinning.

That is the compounding concept. Not more tasks, not more hustle, not more hours. Just less lost time.

When you see work this way, everything changes. Every process becomes a candidate for compression. Every delay is an opportunity. Each task gets closer to the next. The machine runs cleaner.

This is what AI enables for anyone who learns how to use it: not just working harder, but compounding the hours that are already yours.

3

SECOND BRAINS, THIRD HANDS

When people ask what AI really is, I give them this answer. AI is your second brain, and sometimes, your third hand. It does not just help you think. It helps you do.

There is an old productivity metaphor called "clearing the decks." AI clears them before you even reach for a broom.

Consider a senior living facility. You have residents, schedules, maintenance, staffing, and compliance. What used to take ten staff members now takes seven. One of your best employees is invisible, tireless, and cheap. That employee is AI.

One night, I was building out a speech. I did not want to stare at bullet points. I wanted a timeline, visual cues, speaker rhythm—something closer to a mental map. I told ChatGPT, "Take this outline and turn it into a mind map." It did. Then I said, "I need it in org-mode for Emacs." It complied again. I asked, "Build a presentation draft with one paragraph per bullet." In ninety seconds, I had a skeleton keynote.

That is a second brain. That is a creative partner. That is idea-to-output without friction.

Here is where it gets wild.

Suppose you are not building slides, but planning space. You have 1,200 square feet at your facility, and you want to turn it into a tech center for residents. I typed, "Give me a 10-person media room with conferencing capability, list of needed equipment, floor layout, and cost estimate." Five minutes later, I had it all. No architect needed. That is a third hand.

It did not get everything perfect, but it gave me momentum.

That is the power of externalized cognition. AI can remember what you forgot. It can suggest steps you did not know existed. It can show you five versions of a thing you only imagined once.

This is the difference between effort and leverage. Most of us are trained to believe that more output requires more effort. AI flips the math. You give it ten percent of the work, and it fills in the rest with context and inference.

Think about all the little things it can handle. It writes code snippets in Swift or Python. It creates iCal files from university course charts. It summarizes lab results from five years of PDFs. It designs staff schedules with weather, holidays, and fatigue models. It can fill in your daily calories, predict glucose dips, and recommend snacks based on your history.

None of that requires "intelligence" in the human sense. What it requires is connection—between data, tools, and purpose.

That is where the phrase "third hand" comes in. You start throwing repetitive, tactical work at it. AI never gets tired. It never forgets what you asked last week. It builds muscle memory without needing muscles.

This also rewires the creative process. Before AI, most people had to choose between speed and quality. With a second brain, you can sketch ten ideas in the time it used to take to finish one. You can test them. You can throw out nine and still win.

That is not just brainstorming. That is simulation. It is what businesses pay consultants for. Now, it is what you can do at ten p.m. on your couch.

When I was twenty-four, I worked in AI research. Back then, we used languages like Turbo Prolog. We called it "AI," but mostly, it was glorified flowcharts. Then nothing happened for thirty years.

Now, in 2024, AI actually works.

I do not have to pretend anymore. It is not promise. It is presence. It is not theoretical. It is operational.

What it is doing is giving all of us backup cognition. It lets your brain offload what does not matter, so you can focus on what does.

That is the future. Not smarter people. Just more focused ones.

Let AI be your second brain. Let it be your third hand. Then watch what happens to your time.

4

WORKFLOWS VS. TASKS

If you want to understand where AI delivers its real power, stop thinking in terms of tasks. Start thinking in workflows. A task is a to-do item. A workflow is a system that moves something from start to finish, across multiple steps. AI does not just help with the task; it accelerates the flow. That is the shift. If you spend your day crossing off boxes, AI will save you some time. If you spend your day moving ideas through systems, AI will change everything.

Let's get specific. Say you are a healthcare administrator. You get a request to update a staffing model. The old way is to open Excel, search historical data, look at last year's holiday trends, then start dragging cells around. That is a task-based mindset. The new way? You tell GPT, "Using this Excel file, optimize my staffing for weekends, holidays, and known PTO patterns. Prioritize nurses with low fatigue markers from wearable data." It does all of that in seconds. But that only works because the workflow is now digital. When a workflow is digital, it is compressible.

Here is another example. I wanted to research how ambient intelligence is being applied in senior living. I did not go to Google or PubMed. I asked GPT to read five journal articles I uploaded and then summarize them for a board of non-technical healthcare executives. It created a five-hundred-word executive brief, a one-paragraph elevator pitch, and a ten-slide Keynote outline. It even suggested images to match each slide. That is not just time saved. That is workflow collapsed.

Here is what people miss. AI works best when you give it three things: context, purpose, and sequence. That is a workflow. It says, "Here is what I am doing, why I am doing it, and what comes next." Tasks do not have that. Tasks are just isolated actions. If you want AI to feel powerful, stop throwing single-line prompts at it. Feed it a process.

Let's keep going. I had an old coding project I had abandoned, a Swift-based Apple TV app. I could not remember what the original structure was, but I still had the repo. I asked GPT to review the file structure, identify which files controlled navigation, regenerate a project map, and create a roadmap to re-implement using SwiftUI. Ten minutes later, I had a complete resuscitation plan. One task is hard. One workflow is easy.

Why? Because AI loves structure. It thrives in sequence. You give it a pattern, and it finishes the rest. This is true in finance, legal, media, logistics, and engineering. If your job is a chain of micro-decisions, AI can optimize that chain. If your job is a bunch of one-offs, AI can help a little, but not transform it. That is the dividing line. Is your work repeatable? If yes, it is compressible. If not, it is improv theater.

Even creativity follows this rule. Writing this book is not just typing paragraphs. It is outlining, researching, finding anecdotes, drafting, editing, formatting, and exporting. Each part is a step in a workflow. I have AI helping in every stage except the part where I choose which jokes to keep. That is still human. Your job probably breaks down the same way. Once you know your workflows, you can start embedding AI at the friction points. That is the real win. Not replacing yourself, but de-bottlenecking your own systems.

Here is the kicker. Once you do it once, it becomes a template. That is why it compounds. One optimized workflow becomes five. Five become a system. The system starts solving problems before you ask. That is the productivity curve most people never get to. They stop at automation. But automation without workflow understanding is just busier busywork.

If you want to move fast, stop asking, "What can AI do for me?" Start asking, "Where does my work get stuck?" That is your insertion point. That is where AI enters. And that is when your day stops being a checklist and starts becoming a flowchart that runs itself.

PART II

TIME COMPOUNDING: REAL WORK, REAL ROLES

5

NURSES: VOICE-TO-CHART SYSTEMS

My daughter is a nurse in an intensive care unit. Nurses don't get time back. They get what's left over. The typical shift is twelve hours on your feet, balancing dozens of patients, endless documentation, and not enough hours to get it all done. When the day ends, the charting begins. No one likes it, but everyone knows the drill.

This pattern is starting to shift. Hospitals are piloting AI to remove the friction that steals time from nurses and patients alike.

At Northwestern Medicine in Chicago, nurses have trialed ambient voice documentation connected to Epic. While caring for patients, the AI listens and drafts SOAP notes directly into the EHR. Nurses review and approve the note before moving on. At first, it feels unfamiliar. By week's end, it becomes background. Hands are free, notes are completed during the shift, and charting after hours declines. What starts as time compression—removing charting from the end of the day—becomes time compounding. The extra margin lets nurses prep for the next shift, stay ahead on documentation, or simply breathe between rounds.

At Houston Methodist in Texas, bedside tablets equipped with voice recognition are in use. Nurses verbally walk through assessment checklists, and the system converts their responses into structured data fields. If a field is missed, it prompts completion. Unlike the old clipboard routine, nothing gets skipped and compliance improves. These systems were first installed because staffing was short, but over time, they became a scalable form of memory and tracking. The system remembers trends and flags subtle shifts in documentation. For example, when a nurse's daily "no complaints of pain" entry suddenly becomes "mild abdominal discomfort," the AI flags the change for review. The nurse still decides what matters, but the small shifts surface without hunting for them.

Patient education is also evolving. Banner Health in Arizona now embeds an AI assistant on discharge tablets. It reviews medication schedules, delivers post-op instructions, and answers patient questions about wound care or follow-up. Nurses report they spend less time repeating the basics and more time answering the questions that matter. The result is more engaged patients and a measurable dip in readmissions.

Chart summarization has become mobile as well. At the Cleveland Clinic, some nurses are trialing wearable recorders synced with AI summarizers. They tap the device before entering a room, and when they leave, the system drafts a short chart note for review. It is not perfect, but it cuts down on taps and clicks. Over the course of a shift, the savings add up.

Nursing generates more data than almost any other frontline job. Capturing that information used to take longer than collecting the vitals themselves. Now, much of it happens ambiently and invisibly. The value is not automation for its own sake, but the rearrangement of the day into something more breathable.

Charting and compliance still matter. That will not change. What changes is the reclaiming of slices of time that would have been devoured by clicks. Over time, those minutes stack into hours. The hours become confidence, preparation, and momentum.

That is how burnout begins to recede. That is how care improves. Not with more technology, but with less drag.

6

RADIOLOGISTS: FASTER, SAFER SCANS

If you want to see where AI is working—not just theoretically, but operationally—look at radiology.

Radiology has quietly become the most AI-saturated medical specialty. Not because it was easy, but because it was necessary. The volume of scans has exploded. So has image complexity. The number of radiologists? Flat.

That's the perfect recipe for time compression. And that's where AI steps in.

Let me walk you through how.

Aidoc, a company based in Israel, has AI models running in over 900 hospitals. Their tools read CT scans looking for strokes, brain bleeds, pulmonary embolisms—stuff that can't wait. When one of these emergencies shows up, Aidoc jumps the line. It flags the scan for immediate review. No more FIFO queues for life-threatening conditions.

That alone saves lives. But it also saves time. Because it lets radiologists move from batch work to triage mode— putting the worst cases at the top of the pile.

That's not just productivity. That's time compounding.

You've collapsed the wait time, reduced the search time, and avoided delay costs downstream. You've done more than save minutes—you've created an entirely new time geometry for the workflow.

Here's another example: Gold Coast University Hospital in Australia had a backlog of 54,000 unread scans. That's not a typo. Over fifty thousand.

They used AI-powered image prioritization to tear through the stack. The backlog vanished. Turnaround times dropped. Diagnostic accuracy held steady. Nobody got replaced. Everyone got leverage.

Now let's go to the input side. GE Healthcare has embedded AI into some of its X-ray systems. It can detect improper patient positioning before the image is even taken. No more re-dos. No more extra radiation. No more wasted cycles.

That's AI helping at the *start* of the workflow—not the end.

Time compounding happens at both ends. Before the scan is taken and after it's read.

On the reporting side, it gets even better. Tools like Rad AI and CARPL produce draft reads of standard scans. Nothing final—just structured, high-confidence summaries radiologists can review and edit. That alone can reduce reporting time by 20% to 30%, depending on the case type and complexity.

Now multiply that across 100 scans per day. That's a second brain helping a third hand move faster.

This is where the real acceleration begins.

AI doesn't just help a radiologist move faster through one scan. It helps that radiologist see patterns across hundreds of scans. It creates persistent memory. It doesn't fatigue. It doesn't blink.

And if you feed it the right institutional data—like typical pathologies, scanner quirks, and patient demographic patterns—it actually gets better over time. The longer it runs, the more time it returns to you.

That's the definition of time compounding.

You're not just making the same work go faster. You're reducing the need for repeat work. You're reallocating time from "reviewing scan 28" to "catching something in scan 31 that nobody else saw."

Here's something nobody talks about. AI is helping junior radiologists leapfrog the learning curve. It spots what they'd miss. It flags common errors. It trains them as they go. That's AI not just as a tool—but as a tutor.

And when that happens, the team improves. Not just the tech.

That's what I want you to take from this chapter.

AI in radiology isn't about faster scans or better reports. It's about compressing the time between a body entering a machine and a decision being made.

That used to take days. Now it can take minutes.

The quality of care goes up. The cost of delay goes down. And the radiologist gets a shot at doing what they were trained to do: make decisions, not fill out forms.

AI in radiology is time compounding in its purest form. It's not hypothetical. It's here, it's running, and it's quietly saving both lives and hours.

7

HOSPITAL ADMINS: SCHEDULING & THROUGHPUT

Hospital administrators live in spreadsheets. Staffing, patient flow, bed counts, throughput—there's never enough margin, and every variable moves at once.

When you miss a staffing window, the ER backs up. When post-op beds aren't freed fast enough, surgical throughput stalls. It's a cascade of friction, and it eats time.

AI is now being used to manage that friction more like a system—and less like a guessing game.

At Houston Methodist Hospital, an AI tool developed with Epic Systems monitors bed availability, discharge readiness, and staffing in real time. The system predicts when beds will open based on discharge trends and clinical documentation patterns. It flags discharges that are ready but not progressing, so case managers can intervene.

This isn't just reactive reporting. It's anticipatory logistics.

Before the tool, discharge decisions lagged behind real capacity. With the AI layer in place, the hospital increased its bed turnover rate by nearly 15 percent in high-demand wings. That change didn't require new staff. It required better orchestration.

That's how time compounds at scale—by cutting the space between readiness and action.

Now look at operating rooms.

Cedars-Sinai in Los Angeles piloted an AI platform to optimize surgical block scheduling. It used historical case durations, surgeon performance data, and day-of-week patterns to predict true OR time needs. The goal wasn't just to tighten the schedule. It was to reduce over- and under-utilization.

After implementation, unused blocks dropped, and OR idle time decreased by 12 percent. That created space for more procedures—without adding capacity. No new ORs. Just reclaimed time.

In Kansas, Stormont Vail Health implemented Qventus, an AI-driven hospital operations platform. It helped manage staffing and patient flow in their medical-surgical units. The platform absorbed data from the EHR and internal logistics systems, then made staffing suggestions based on predicted volume spikes.

What used to require three nurse managers and a spreadsheet each morning now runs as a live dashboard. Staffing mismatches fell. Cross-unit shifts decreased. Staff burnout improved slightly—not dramatically, but enough to notice.

The time savings weren't loud. They accumulated.

That's the pattern across hospital ops AI: quiet efficiency. The kind that doesn't show up in marketing brochures, but that department heads notice after three months.

Even patient transport is getting AI assistance. Mount Sinai in New York tested a dispatch optimization tool to reduce the wait time between discharge orders and actual transport. Previously, transport delays created backlogs at critical choke points—PACU, ED, telemetry.

With AI routing in place, average wait time dropped from 50 minutes to 22. That created measurable flow relief across the care continuum. It also shortened length of stay metrics in borderline cases, which added billing flexibility.

One senior administrator there said it plainly during a panel: "We didn't need new staff. We needed better timing." That's the core of it. Hospitals aren't just short on people. They're short on alignment.

AI doesn't fill empty roles. But it cuts the coordination lag between teams. And when that lag goes away, everything else starts to move.

Across the board, these systems don't work because they're smart. They work because they're synchronized. Data is pulled into one place, processed faster, and turned into action before someone asks.

That's where time gets compounded in hospital operations—not through automation, but through acceleration of the middle layer: readiness, routing, resource use.

Each day runs slightly tighter. Each discharge goes slightly smoother. And the cumulative effect, over months, is systemic slack that didn't exist before.

Hospitals don't need more dashboards. They need fewer delays between knowing something and doing something. That's what this layer of AI is finally starting to deliver.

8

SENIOR CARE: UNDER PRESSURE

If there's one industry that can't afford wasted time, it's senior care. Staff are short, documentation is heavy, and small mistakes have big consequences. The work is constant, but the real currency is time.

AI is starting to fix that.

In Florida, a mid-sized senior living facility piloted a voice-based digital assistant named Nuri. Residents used it to request medication reminders, report room issues, and ask health questions. The system handled about 40 percent of inbound requests from residents. That meant nurses got fewer interruptions and could focus on the residents who truly needed them.

The real value? Nuri didn't just answer questions. It learned patterns. One resident asked about blood pressure every morning. Eventually, the system flagged the trend and alerted a nurse to investigate. That's not just automation. That's time redeployed before a health issue escalated.

In Illinois, a company trialed a fall-risk detection system using computer vision. It didn't just track movement. It learned gait patterns over time, identifying when residents began walking differently. The staff got alerts hours or days before an actual fall. This didn't just prevent injury. It saved the hours of paperwork, observation, and follow-up that come after every incident.

One administrator told me the time savings were subtle at first. Then they stacked. Fewer injuries meant fewer reports. Fewer reports meant less time on compliance calls. Less compliance time meant more hours back on the floor. This is what compounding time looks like in practice: nothing flashy, just a steady removal of drag.

Cognitive support is another area that's shifting. A facility in Oregon is testing a generative language model that offers conversation starters to residents with early-stage dementia. The AI listens and responds in the resident's preferred rhythm and tone. It doesn't pretend to be human. But it keeps them engaged long enough for staff to prepare meals, tend to others, or catch their breath.

Time isn't just saved. It's rearranged into better sequences.

Let's talk documentation. It used to take one facility's head nurse 90 minutes a day to fill out care logs. With a lightweight AI summarizer integrated into her mobile device, she dictates notes while walking between rooms. Now it takes 20 minutes. She doesn't go home late anymore. That's a win.

The AI didn't do anything miraculous. It just compressed the structure of a day. That's where all the time is hiding—in transitions, in workflows, in repeated steps that nobody has time to question.

And no, this doesn't mean the job is getting easier. The human part is still hard. But when AI clears away the repetitive junk, the people doing the real work get to breathe. They get to do their jobs better. That shows up in morale, turnover, and resident experience.

Some of this is new. Some of it is obvious. But it's happening now, not in a lab, and not in some $10,000-per-month facility. Mid-market operators are the ones experimenting, mostly out of necessity.

What they're learning is simple. AI doesn't give them more people. But it gives their people more reach. That's enough.

That's how time starts to compound in senior care—not with bold claims, but with fewer slips, shorter nights, and more attention where it matters.

Similarly, in Sweden, an AI system was implemented across public primary care facilities to automate the triage process and support clinical decision-making. The system uses a Bayesian network framework to assess patient information and recommend appropriate care pathways. Early results indicate improved efficiency and patient satisfaction.

These systems don't just process information faster—they learn over time. With each interaction, they refine their algorithms, leading to more accurate triage decisions and better resource allocation.

That's time compounding in action.

Every minute saved on administrative tasks is a minute gained for patient care. Over days, weeks, and months, these savings accumulate, allowing clinicians to see more patients, spend more time on complex cases, and reduce burnout.

But AI's impact isn't limited to triage and referrals.

In the realm of chronic disease management, AI tools are helping primary care providers monitor patients more effectively. For instance, some platforms analyze patient data to identify those at risk of conditions like diabetes or hypertension. They then generate personalized care plans and reminders, ensuring proactive management and reducing the likelihood of complications.

Moreover, AI-driven chatbots are being used to provide patients with 24/7 access to health information and support. These virtual assistants can answer common questions, schedule appointments, and even provide mental health support, freeing up staff time and improving patient engagement.

Of course, challenges remain.

Data privacy, algorithm transparency, and the need for human oversight are critical considerations. AI should augment, not replace, clinical judgment.

But when implemented thoughtfully, AI becomes a force multiplier.

It doesn't just make primary care faster—it makes it smarter.

By automating routine tasks, prioritizing urgent cases, and supporting clinical decisions, AI allows primary care providers to focus on what they do best: caring for patients.

In a world where demand often outpaces supply, that's not just helpful—that's transformative.

9

EDUCATION: PERSONALIZED LEARNING AT SCALE

Teachers aren't short on effort. They're short on hours.

Every minute spent grading, prepping, or tracking attendance is a minute pulled from actual teaching. Multiply that across five classes, thirty students per room, and a school year that never feels long enough. Then layer in burnout.

AI isn't going to fix education. But it's already starting to compress the parts of the job that don't need to be manual anymore.

Start with lesson planning. In Michigan, a middle school science teacher uses a prompt-based lesson generator. She types: "Design a five-day unit on volcanoes aligned with 6th grade NGSS standards, include a hands-on lab." Thirty seconds later, she has an outline, a materials list, and printable worksheets. She still edits them, of course. But she's no longer starting from scratch.

Her prep time went from two hours to thirty minutes. That's not just faster. That's reclaimed bandwidth.

Now zoom out. One district in North Carolina started feeding anonymized standardized test data into a learning model to identify where students were falling behind. The AI sorted students by concept mastery, then recommended differentiated instruction strategies for each tier. Teachers weren't surprised by who struggled—they were surprised by how early the AI spotted it.

The intervention window widened. Teachers could now act before the report card did the talking.

That's time compounding in education: giving back minutes today that prevent hours of remediation tomorrow.

And it's not just the teachers gaining time. Students are too.

In Texas, a rural high school is using an AI-powered reading coach for students with dyslexia. The system reads aloud, highlights passages, and responds to voice commands. One student who had refused to read in class now logs in early. The teacher says he's gone from avoidance to autonomy.

Meanwhile, a charter school in Arizona uses AI to personalize math problem sets daily. Each student gets five new problems based on yesterday's performance. If they breeze through, the next batch gets harder. If they struggle, the next set backs off and inserts a hint. The system runs silently in the background, adapting in real time. No labels. No judgment. Just frictionless scaffolding.

In a speech you gave at a university board retreat, you said, "AI isn't replacing teachers. It's just filling in the blanks they don't have time to fill." That line stuck with me while writing this chapter. Because it gets at the real value here. AI doesn't inspire students. But it gives teachers space to try.

Let's go back to grading.

An English teacher in Oregon uses an AI assistant to provide first-pass feedback on essays. The AI flags unclear arguments, repeated phrases, and passive constructions. The teacher still reviews every paper. But now he sees patterns earlier. He builds mini-lessons around the most common issues.

That's what happens when you compress the review cycle: you catch the drift before it becomes a habit.

Some of the best use cases are invisible. A superintendent in Colorado uses AI to track district-wide attendance trends, correlate them with test performance, and generate weekly alerts. It takes her 10 minutes each Friday. It used to take her two days a month.

Nobody gets excited about dashboards. But they work.

The trick with education isn't to automate instruction. It's to make room for it.

AI can't teach empathy. It can't replace the instinct a teacher has when they know a student is struggling but won't say it. What it can do is reduce the noise around that moment, so the teacher can hear it.

This chapter could've been full of bold claims and startup names. But the real story is in the hours saved, the moments noticed, and the gaps closed.

That's where the time compounds. Quietly. Relentlessly. Where it's needed most.

10

LITIGATORS: RAPID CASE PREP

Litigation moves slowly—until it doesn't. One minute you're reviewing documents, the next you're prepping a witness, writing a motion, and racing toward trial.

Time gets burned on document review, case chronology, deposition indexing, and expert vetting. The real legal work often starts after the clerical work is done.

AI is shortening that lag.

At Winston & Strawn, a major litigation firm, lawyers are using a proprietary GPT-based system trained on the firm's internal briefs, filings, and memos. It doesn't just summarize a case; it drafts first-pass arguments in the firm's own voice. The tool can assemble procedural history and legal positioning based on uploaded pleadings and evidence logs.

Before, that took an associate six hours. Now it's a three-minute process. The associate still rewrites—but they're starting from a position, not a pile of PDFs.

That's time compression. But once the system is trained and refined, it becomes part of a repeatable chain.

That's where time starts to compound.

Another firm, Allen & Overy, has embedded Harvey AI across their litigation group. The tool assists with identifying precedent, summarizing testimony, and proposing draft responses to common procedural motions. It sits inside their daily stack—Teams, Outlook, Word.

They don't ask it for opinions. They ask it to save them the first three rounds of thinking.

For deposition prep, a growing number of firms now use AI to scan witness transcripts, tag inconsistencies, and compare testimony against established case timelines. One platform, Luminance, has built this capability into their litigation module. Firms feed in chronologies and document sets, and the system flags inconsistencies across depositions and filings.

What used to require a summer associate building a timeline in Excel now happens with a drag-and-drop interface.

The gain isn't just speed. It's early insight. When inconsistencies get flagged in the first week, litigation strategy shifts sooner. That's not just compounding time. That's war-gaming ahead of schedule.

Several eDiscovery platforms have layered in generative summaries. Relativity, for example, can now draft narratives from clustered documents. A 12,000-document trove becomes a four-page summary with citations to key exhibits.

Lawyers aren't skipping the documents. They're triaging smarter. The result? More time for deposition strategy and expert vetting. Less time spent labeling attachments and sorting through ten copies of the same boilerplate email.

Firms are even starting to automate privilege review. Tools like Everlaw and DISCO use machine learning models to detect patterns in privileged communication. One BigLaw case team reported a 40% drop in false-positive flags after deploying an adaptive model mid-case.

That saved more than time. It saved embarrassment.

None of this replaces judgment. But it removes the friction between data and decision-making. That's what high-leverage AI does.

It's not that the work disappears. It's that the sequence changes.

The first 40% of a case—document prep, timeline reconciliation, issue tagging—gets compressed. Which means the remaining 60% gets richer. More iteration. More angles. More time spent testing arguments instead of formatting them.

One managing partner said publicly that they've cut first-round motion drafting time by half. Not by writing less. By preparing better.

Litigation used to reward firms that could throw bodies at a problem. Now it's shifting toward firms that know how to layer tools into the grind.

That doesn't make the work easier. It makes the strategic phase start sooner.

Which, in this business, is everything.

11

CONTRACT LAWYERS: CLAUSE DETECTION & SUGGESTION

Contract work is where legal time often goes to die. Reviewing NDAs, redlining service agreements, flagging indemnity language—it's repetitive, detail-heavy, and risk-sensitive. And most of it doesn't scale.

AI is changing that, especially at the clause level.

Ironclad, a contract lifecycle platform, now includes AI-powered clause detection across hundreds of contract types. Their Smart Import tool reads contracts and highlights non-standard language in indemnification, termination, and limitation-of-liability clauses. Legal teams can build playbooks that tag anything outside preferred risk tolerances.

One general counsel at a fintech firm reported that first-pass review time dropped by over 60% after deploying

Ironclad's clause intelligence layer. Junior lawyers stopped flagging everything. They started flagging what mattered.

That's not just faster work. That's cleaner triage. And it accumulates.

LegalOn, another platform gaining traction in midsize firms, focuses on "legal hygiene." Its AI checks contracts for missing clauses, contradictory terms, and unbalanced obligations. It doesn't generate text—it highlights gaps.

Think of it as preventive maintenance for contracts.

One enterprise user fed the system 200 vendor agreements. The AI found 26 with missing data protection clauses—contracts that would've otherwise slipped through to execution. Those flags prevented downstream compliance risk. But more importantly, they prevented the follow-up legal work those gaps would've created.

That's time compounding in contract law: mistakes not made mean fires not fought.

Large firms are also adapting. Clifford Chance has integrated proprietary clause libraries with Kira Systems' NLP engine. When a new contract arrives, the system compares every clause to the firm's benchmark set. It assigns confidence scores to each variation and flags anything unusual.

The review lawyer starts with the exceptions—not the whole document.

That reorders the workload. It doesn't shrink it. But it changes the starting line.

ContractPodAi offers another layer. Their platform uses GPT-style models to suggest fallback clauses during negotiation. If a third party strikes your governing law clause, the system recommends alternatives aligned with internal policy—already pre-approved.

That turns what used to be a Slack ping to legal into a click.

At scale, this reduces review cycles by 25–35% depending on contract type. The biggest gains happen in high-volume settings: procurement, tech licensing, vendor onboarding.

Even compliance is getting compressed. SpotDraft, a contract ops tool, integrates with Salesforce to monitor deal timelines. If a contract has stalled, it flags where in the process—usually redlines, missing approvals, or clause conflicts. It lets legal ops fix delays before they become complaints.

That saves more than time. It saves trust.

AI isn't making contract law simple. It's making the basic layers more navigable. The human part still handles nuance. But the system handles the 80% of clauses that repeat, recur, and waste time when done manually.

And when those get flagged, routed, and resolved faster, the lawyer's role shifts. Less cleanup. More strategy.

That's what this chapter is about. Not better redlines. Better sequencing.

When review starts with anomaly detection, not brute-force reading, time stops being something you spend. It becomes something you structure.

And that's where leverage lives.

12

SOLO PRACTITIONERS: AI AS A PARALEGAL

Most solo lawyers aren't running firms. They're running triage centers.

Client intake, scheduling, research, invoicing, filings—everything lands on one desk. The lawyer does the work. The lawyer files the motion. The lawyer sends the invoice. Then they go to court and start again.

It's not about being inefficient. It's about bandwidth.

That's why AI hits different here. Not as an assistant, but as infrastructure.

Take CoCounsel by Casetext, now part of Thomson Reuters. It's trained specifically for legal reasoning and document review. Solo practitioners use it to summarize discovery documents, draft interrogatories, and extract factual timelines from depositions. Instead of combing through a 300-page exhibit dump, a lawyer can pull the who-what-when in a paragraph.

That's not a shortcut. That's re-sequencing prep so the lawyer walks into court with context—before the opposing side even starts discovery.

In North Carolina, a family law attorney feeds her intake forms into Spellbook, a contract drafting assistant that now supports limited court forms. The AI auto-generates draft parenting plans and calculates equitable distribution schedules based on client input.

She still checks everything. But the bulk of formatting and copy-pasting is gone. What used to take four hours now takes one. She sees more clients per week, but works fewer nights.

That's how time starts to compound. Not by doing less work, but by lowering the threshold to start it.

Solo lawyers also use AI for client communication. One small practice in California uses a GPT-based system trained on prior client emails. It drafts first-pass responses for billing, document requests, or procedural updates. The lawyer still reviews each one. But the replies are no longer blank screens.

Even if it only saves three minutes per email, across 30 emails a day, it becomes a second hour. That hour gets spent on prep, strategy, or sleep. All of which matter.

BriefPoint.ai, another new tool, automatically generates legal briefs based on uploaded complaints and statutes. It's being used in small claims and traffic courts, where volume is high and margins are razor-thin. Solo lawyers get a draft that's 70% usable in 30 seconds.

The result isn't perfect. But it's directional. And it's enough to break the inertia that often slows small-firm work.

Billing automation is another time sink being eroded. Smokeball, a practice management suite for solos and small firms, tracks work inside Microsoft Word and Outlook, and applies hourly rates in the background. Lawyers used to miss 20–30% of billable hours just by forgetting to log them. Now they recover that time automatically.

It's not about squeezing clients. It's about not losing what was already earned.

Even court filing is shifting. Services like Lawyaw offer AI-generated forms that adapt to jurisdictional requirements. That removes the need to keep a private stash of county-specific PDFs and outdated templates. One solo bankruptcy attorney said the platform saved him 10–12 hours per week on form prep alone.

That time didn't vanish. It got moved. He now uses it for actual client calls.

The legal system hasn't gotten simpler. But the solo firm now has leverage it never had before.

The paralegal, the receptionist, the junior associate— they're all built into the stack. And while AI won't argue the motion or shake hands with a client, it builds enough runway that the lawyer has time to do both.

In solo practice, time is usually the constraint. AI changes that constraint into a margin.

It doesn't make the work easier. It makes it flow.

13

WEALTH ADVISORS: PERSONALIZED PORTFOLIOS IN SECONDS

Wealth advisors used to compete on access. Now they compete on responsiveness.

Clients don't want market updates—they already get those from apps. What they want is context, delivered fast, and tailored to their situation. The problem is, real personalization takes time. Or at least, it used to.

AI is turning that time drag into leverage.

Schwab's Advisor Center now includes AI-generated portfolio insights. Advisors get suggestions on rebalancing, tax-loss harvesting, and risk drift in seconds. Instead of pulling reports, running ratios, and drafting summaries, the advisor opens a dashboard that already highlights where action is needed.

The human still makes the call. But they don't waste time building the map. It's already drawn.

Vise, a New York-based platform, pushes this even further. It builds and rebalances custom portfolios for RIAs based on client profiles. The advisor defines objectives and constraints, and Vise handles trade execution and optimization. If a client changes their risk profile, the AI retools the portfolio overnight.

What once took a committee and an Excel model now runs in the background.

The time savings compound because they're front-loaded. Every decision starts with a ready state. And the fewer steps between idea and execution, the more bandwidth the advisor has to focus on trust, not toggling.

TIFIN Wealth, another platform in the space, delivers personalized behavioral finance nudges. It detects when a client is prone to overreacting to volatility and flags it to the advisor. The message is personalized, calm, and pre-written. The advisor reviews, then clicks send.

The advisor didn't spend 30 minutes writing that email. They spent 30 seconds deciding whether to send it. That's a different job entirely.

And it keeps clients from panicking out of the market. Which preserves value. Which saves time cleaning up after bad decisions.

AI isn't just changing the work. It's changing when the work begins.

Advyzon, an all-in-one RIA platform, uses predictive analytics to surface clients who may be under-engaged. It recommends outreach based on portfolio drift, time since last contact, and life event indicators. Advisors say it's helped them identify accounts heading toward churn —early enough to reengage.

That's time compounded as retention. Minutes spent reaching out now prevent hours spent rebuilding later.

Some firms are even automating prospect analysis. Snappy Kraken, a marketing automation platform for advisors, integrates AI-generated client personas with campaign suggestions. If a potential client downloads a guide on 401(k) rollovers, the system queues a targeted follow-up sequence. The advisor doesn't manage the funnel. They manage the timing.

It's not just CRM. It's CRM that thinks ahead.

The compliance side is tightening too. Orion Advisor Tech integrates AI to monitor for messaging inconsistencies across advisor-client communication. It flags language that could trigger regulatory review. That used to be a full-time job in large firms. Now it's part of the stack.

Fewer mistakes. Less cleanup. More flow.

And at the high end, multi-family offices are now building GPT-powered tools trained on their own house views. These internal copilots summarize earnings reports, draft quarterly commentary, and surface talking points before client meetings. Advisors don't rely on them for judgment. But they use them to prep faster and show up sharper.

That's not automation. That's compounding attention.

The common thread is time—less of it wasted, more of it reinvested in signal over noise. Advisors don't need help managing portfolios. They need help managing focus.

AI doesn't replace judgment. It just gets everything ready before the meeting starts.

That's the edge now. Not who knows the most, but who gets to the decision first.

14

INVESTMENT RESEARCH ANALYSTS: EARNINGS PREP AND REPORT GENERATION

Equity analysts are supposed to be early. Early with the take, early with the reaction, early with the interpretation of what this quarter means. But when everyone's running the same models and reading the same transcripts, timing alone isn't enough.

AI is giving analysts an earlier start—not by offering better opinions, but by compressing the lead-up to them.

At UBS and Morgan Stanley, large language models trained on decades of transcripts now produce first-pass earnings summaries before the call ends. They highlight changes in guidance language, management tone, and the competitive landscape. These summaries land in dashboards that update in real time as the call proceeds.

Instead of listening first and thinking second, the analyst now thinks while the call is still happening.

That doesn't just save time. It shifts when insight begins.

AlphaSense and FinChat extend this by processing filings, presentations, and press releases. These tools build valuation tables and draft reaction notes within minutes. Analysts review and edit—but they start from a structured draft, not a blank slide.

Time compounds when the first 70% of the job disappears.

Bridgewater uses internal models to map macro dependencies across sectors and asset classes. If Ford misses on margins, the system flags potential input cost problems for other auto manufacturers and capital goods firms. This used to require an experienced analyst tracking eight companies and reading four calls a day. Now it's surfaced instantly.

Research becomes anticipatory. That's what time compression makes possible.

FactSet and Refinitiv offer tone analytics APIs. Analysts can see how a CEO's confidence score has trended over five quarters, or when language related to pricing power gets more cautious. These are subtle shifts—but they're now measurable.

That used to be gut. Now it's data. And data moves faster.

Valuation models have also changed. GPT-style systems can pull three years of financials, apply a comp set, and generate base-case and bear-case projections within minutes. Analysts don't rely on this for accuracy. They rely on it to get to the real work sooner.

Pitch decks have followed. Tegus and YCharts now create draft slide sets based on earnings data. Analysts used to spend four hours building slides, double-checking numbers, and formatting charts. Now that structure is auto-generated. The analyst still controls the story. But the scaffolding arrives finished.

That saves more than time. It saves cognitive energy that would have gone into formatting instead of framing.

On the client side, GPT-trained writing assistants now draft summary emails in firm-specific language. Compliance still reviews them. But the difference is speed—and consistency. Every client gets a message within 30 minutes of the call. That used to take all afternoon.

Clients stay ahead of their peers. That's retention.

None of this changes the core skill of research. Analysts still need to identify the real delta, frame the impact, and guide the narrative. But now, every part of the workflow that didn't require judgment is handled in advance.

And that makes the judgment sharper. It lands faster. It's supported by structure instead of buried beneath it.

AI isn't writing the note. It's building the desk it sits on.

Time compounds in research when the analyst begins at relevance, not review.

That's where insight actually starts.

15

PRIVATE EQUITY: DILIGENCE, MODELING, AND MONITORING

Private equity isn't slow by accident. It's slow by necessity. Every step—sourcing, diligence, modeling, deal structuring—is sequential. If one link drags, the whole deal slips. What AI is bringing to this world isn't shortcuts. It's compression of the in-between.

Top-of-funnel sourcing is being reworked first. Firms like SourceScrub and Grata use AI to scan, score, and filter companies by headcount, revenue trajectory, M&A activity, and industry fit. The old way—manual screening, industry conferences, and cold lists—kept analysts mired in research. Now the pipeline is pre-scored, and the analyst starts with context, not chaos.

Diligence is getting its own kind of overhaul. Bain Capital and KKR deploy natural language models trained on legal docs and contracts. The AI parses NDAs, customer lists, vendor agreements, and flag clauses outside of norms—change of control, early termination, exclusivity, indemnity. Human counsel still does the real reading. But the drift is caught before it spreads.

Modeling is where time really compounds. Fathom, Cyndx, and Jirav ingest P&Ls, balance sheets, and operating metrics, and produce base case, downside, and M&A scenario models. Partners no longer wait for associates to adjust twenty assumptions by hand. The AI does the heavy lift. The team refines instead of resets.

Iteration, once a bottleneck, is now fluid. Partners can test five scenarios before lunch, not by the end of the week.

After close, portfolio monitoring is a second frontier. Palantir Foundry and similar platforms aggregate accounting, sales, and workforce data. Alerts are set for margin compression, revenue slip, cash burn, and executive turnover. Instead of waiting for quarterly board decks, partners see the trouble forming in real time.

Even talent management is getting compressed. PE-backed companies feed HR data into AI models that flag flight risks, succession gaps, and comp outliers. No one replaces human relationships. But departures don't blindside the firm.

On the investor side, LP communication is accelerating. GPT-style tools draft investor letters, pipeline updates, and deal summaries in the firm's house language. Compliance still signs off, but the first draft lands days sooner. When investors ask for pipeline visibility, the team generates updates from CRM logs—already sorted by sector, stage, and deal velocity.

The real power here isn't speed. It's sequence. The next step starts while the last one finishes.

Deal teams don't skip steps. They compress the downtime between them. Sourcing runs tighter. Diligence finds red flags before the data room closes. Modeling answers more questions, faster. Portfolio monitoring surfaces trouble while there's still time to act.

Private equity will never be about speed. It will always be about reducing risk in layers. But when those layers stack closer together, the flywheel spins faster and with less drag.

AI isn't making judgment unnecessary. It's making the road to judgment frictionless.

Partners still negotiate, still interpret, still pull the trigger. But every part of the process that isn't judgment—screening, cross-checking, updating, flagging—now lands in the background.

The pace of private equity is deliberate. But now, deliberate doesn't have to mean slow.

Time compounds when rigor keeps its rhythm.

That's the new tempo for the best firms in the business.

16

INSURANCE: CLAIMS, RISK MODELS, AND FRAUD DETECTION

Insurance was built on delay. Every claim, policy, and premium had to pass through layers of paperwork, reviews, and approvals. Some called it prudence. Others called it friction. Either way, time was the currency— and the cost.

AI hasn't removed risk from insurance. It's just started to re-sequence how and when it's measured.

Claims processing, for instance, was long known for its paperwork. Lemonade, the digital-first insurer, made headlines for using AI-powered bots to handle basic claims. When a policyholder files for a stolen bike, the system reviews the claim, checks policy rules, and often pays out within minutes. The exceptions—where fraud or complexity is likely—are routed to human adjusters.

It's not perfect. There are disputes, and there are times when automation gets it wrong. But for standard cases, the time savings are real. Claims that took weeks now close in an afternoon.

Traditional insurers are responding with their own layers of automation. Allstate's QuickFoto Claim lets customers upload accident photos; an AI model assesses damage, compares it to historical claims, and generates a settlement estimate. The adjuster still reviews, but their work begins at a different point—closer to resolution than to intake.

Risk modeling is another area getting compressed. Swiss Re and Munich Re both use AI-driven catastrophe models that integrate weather feeds, satellite data, and local infrastructure inputs. Instead of waiting for the next season's reinsurance pricing, underwriters adjust their models as new data lands. Risk isn't static; it's recalibrated in near-real time.

Of course, not all risks can be measured by algorithms. That's the hard part. Sometimes the model misses the long tail, or overcorrects for noise. But as the models improve, more of the mundane is handled upfront— leaving underwriters to focus on nuance.

Fraud detection is where the benefits are less abstract. Shift Technology and FRISS analyze claims data for behavioral anomalies: mismatched addresses, repeated incident patterns, or claims filed just after new policies take effect. They flag these for review before payout.

Insurers say that not every flag is a fraud. Sometimes, it's just a customer in a hurry. But the system lets human adjusters spend their time where it matters most—on the ambiguous, the rare, the genuine outlier.

Underwriting workflows are also accelerating. Hippo and Root use AI to ingest public records, property imagery, and IoT device data. Instead of waiting on manual inspections, underwriters approve or price policies with a few clicks. That makes the customer journey smoother—and the book of business more current.

This isn't a revolution. There are still gaps, mistakes, and edge cases where human review is essential. But the old rhythm—wait, review, refer, repeat—is changing. Now, action comes earlier, and the hardest work is reserved for where it's needed most.

Even regulatory compliance, once a maze of forms and approvals, is shifting. Insurers use natural language models to scan policy language for state-by-state variations, catching compliance problems before regulators do.

Time compounds in insurance not because there are fewer steps, but because the slow steps shrink and the fast steps stack up. Claims get paid sooner, risks get priced tighter, and fraud gets flagged earlier in the cycle.

Maybe we're not at the end of insurance friction. But for the first time in decades, the industry's relationship to time is changing.

And for customers, brokers, and underwriters alike, that's a shift worth noting.

17

TRADERS: SIGNAL EXTRACTION AND PORTFOLIO REBALANCING

Traders used to rely on instinct, speed, and screens. Each edge came from seeing something before someone else did—anomalous volume, implied volatility spikes, ETF lag. Then came saturation. Every terminal showed the same information, and every desk traded it in parallel.

AI has changed that. Not by replacing traders, but by rerouting how trades develop. Speed is no longer the edge. Sequence is.

At Citadel and Two Sigma, machine learning systems are trained to surface correlations that don't show up in traditional models. Instead of tracking single indicators, these systems process large multi-factor environments:

when rate hikes coincide with currency softness and energy prices stabilize, some specific equity pairs outperform. That pattern might not recur for a year. But when it does, the model sees it first.

This doesn't just shorten research. It redefines it. Analysts still interrogate the thesis. But the starting point is built from signal density, not screens.

Execution is being restructured too. JPMorgan's LOXM platform uses reinforcement learning to route large orders across venues. It adjusts to fill quality, latency, and spread dynamics in real time. Before AI, this level of micromanagement had to be done manually—splitting orders, watching dark pools, hoping for no slippage.

Now the model learns from past performance and adjusts on the fly. What used to take constant monitoring happens invisibly. The desk sees better execution without knowing how it was shaped.

Retail traders feel this shift in different ways. Platforms like Robinhood, eToro, and TradingView now offer "unusual activity" feeds, heat maps, and sentiment overlays. These are machine-sorted summaries of what used to require a Bloomberg terminal and 40 minutes of digging.

Time compounds here by removing scavenger work. The trader doesn't search. The system highlights. They decide.

Rebalancing, once the province of quarterly models, is now continuous. Wealthfront and Betterment deploy AI to monitor drift, harvest tax losses, and reinvest proceeds. Adjustments happen automatically and incrementally. Small moves are made daily to avoid large, costly ones later.

The trader doesn't initiate the rebalance. They review the portfolio and see that it's already tighter than expected.

Time doesn't just get saved. It gets quietly redistributed.

AI-native funds like Numerai integrate crowd-sourced strategies into a single ensemble. Thousands of submitted models are blended, scored, and adjusted based on live return profiles. No single trader runs the strategy—yet the system itself evolves continuously, learning what works under current volatility and trend regimes.

Traditional hedge funds can't iterate that quickly. What took three months of live testing is now tested overnight.

Signal processing has advanced as well. Firms like Kensho and Dataminr use natural language models to scan news, speeches, and filings. They flag when sentiment shifts or regulatory language tightens. The trader gets a headline and a confidence score—not a deluge of RSS feeds.

That means conviction builds faster. Not recklessly, but from a smaller pool of filtered inputs.

Options traders now have access to implied volatility curves, skew anomalies, and gamma exposure visualizations updated live by AI models. At firms like QVR Advisors, these tools enable pre-hedging and asymmetric positioning ahead of market makers adjusting.

That used to require reading the tape. Now it's a dashboard.

None of this removes the need for strategy. It just removes the lag.

What AI does best here is compress the non-decision parts of trading. The part where you used to load charts, write code, watch flows, and try to spot shape in noise. That's not where decisions are made. That's where time was lost.

Now the model does that. The trader reads what matters and moves.

Edge hasn't disappeared. It's just been rerouted through faster structure.

And in modern markets, that structure is the only thing fast enough to matter.

18

MORTGAGE BROKERS: LOAN ORIGINATION AND BORROWER AUTOMATION

Mortgage brokers used to be translators. They'd gather paperwork, explain rate sheets, bridge gaps between lenders and anxious borrowers, and chase signatures across kitchen tables. The bottleneck wasn't knowledge. It was the sequence—each step waiting on the last.

AI is shifting those steps forward, sometimes compressing the whole process into a single workflow.

Blend, a digital mortgage platform, uses AI-driven data extraction to pull pay stubs, bank statements, and tax records automatically. Applicants upload documents once. The system parses, verifies, and fills in the mortgage application, flagging anomalies for review. This isn't a one-click loan, but it's a world away from fax machines and photocopiers.

That front-end compression changes everything down-stream. Brokers no longer spend half their day chasing missing forms or correcting typos. Instead, they start with a completed file and focus on the hard parts: edge cases, non-W-2 income, complex property types.

Ellie Mae (now ICE Mortgage Technology) integrates automated underwriting models that cross-check application data against lender risk models and regulatory compliance rules. Instead of waiting days for manual review, borrowers receive conditional approvals in minutes, not weeks.

Time compounds when approvals land before anxiety builds. Deals move forward before the borrower loses interest or shops elsewhere.

Rocket Mortgage and Better Mortgage use natural language chatbots to answer questions, schedule calls, and walk applicants through disclosures. Instead of leaving voicemails and waiting hours for a callback, clients get responses in real time, twenty-four hours a day.

The broker's bandwidth stretches further. Routine questions are offloaded to the system, freeing up time for rate negotiation and relationship building.

Even document collection is changing. Ocrolus and Plaid connect directly to banks and payroll providers, verifying assets and income at the source. The borrower doesn't have to download, print, and scan statements. The system pulls live data, flags inconsistencies, and updates the file.

That's fewer abandoned applications and fewer surprises at closing.

On the back end, automated compliance review tools now scan files for missing signatures, disclosure gaps, and potential violations. Errors that used to trigger delays on closing day are flagged the week before. Brokers spend less time on remediation and more time prepping the next file.

Some lenders are using AI to forecast close probability and rate lock risk. The model tracks pipeline age, borrower responsiveness, and local market velocity. If a loan is likely to fall through, the broker knows early— sometimes early enough to save the deal or focus efforts elsewhere.

This shift isn't perfect. Automated models sometimes miss nuances in self-employment income or unusual credit events. There are edge cases where the system can't deliver. But those become the exception, not the norm.

For most brokers, this means more deals in less time, with more predictable timelines. Stress comes less from paperwork bottlenecks and more from actual deal complexity. That's a trade most will make.

Clients benefit, too. The process feels more transparent and responsive. Borrowers don't wonder where their file is—they can check status, upload missing documents, or sign disclosures from their phone.

The real change is in the tempo. Where once a loan could stall for days between steps, now the process advances whenever data lands. Brokers spend less time as clerks and more as advisors.

AI isn't removing the mortgage broker. It's freeing them from the waiting room.

And in a market where deals die in the lag, that speed is often the difference between closed and lost.

CoreLogic, a data provider widely used by appraisers, integrates natural language models to scan for recent code changes, permitting delays, and environmental risk. The system highlights variances from local trends and flags outliers for closer review.

Time compounds when the easy work is cleared out. The professional's energy shifts to judgment calls instead of rote form-filling.

Even municipal appraisal departments are changing tempo. New York City's Department of Finance uses AI-driven mass appraisal to monitor shifting valuations across neighborhoods. When market heat or cools, the model flags sectors for reassessment. It doesn't replace local expertise—but it gives the appraiser a signal where to dig.

The same logic applies in commercial property. REalyse and Bowery Valuation use predictive analytics to benchmark office, retail, and multifamily assets. The model surfaces comparable leases, highlights vacancy risk, and provides a baseline value that's updated daily. Appraisers review, but they do not start from zero.

This speeds up not just the individual report, but the entire queue of pending work.

Lenders benefit too. Fannie Mae and Freddie Mac have integrated AVMs to reduce unnecessary full appraisals. If the property matches low-risk profiles, and the comp range is tight, the deal proceeds with an appraisal waiver. When the numbers don't align, the job goes to a human for a deeper dive.

That means the appraiser spends less time on cookie-cutter deals and more time on edge cases.

Quality control is also getting compressed. Valcre and other workflow tools automate error checking, form compliance, and client delivery. Fewer reports bounce for missing signatures or data mismatches. Review cycles shorten. Corrections happen before the client sees the first draft.

This isn't the end of appraisals. It's a reshuffling of the job. The friction that once filled a day is now background. The work that remains is harder, but also higher value.

There are still gaps. Automated models sometimes miss interior renovations or local quirks. No system can see the custom kitchen hidden behind an unchanged exterior photo. The professional appraiser still decides when the model is out of its depth.

But the sequence has shifted. Time that was lost to driving, data entry, and duplicate research now lands in judgment, investigation, and review.

For the best appraisers, this means more work in less time, and more focus on the questions that actually demand expertise.

That's where AI's impact is most clear: shifting attention from the obvious to the important.

And in real estate valuation, that's the only way to keep up.

19

ACCOUNTANTS: RECONCILIATIONS ON AUTOPILOT

Reconciliation used to be the part of accounting you pushed to Friday. Or the 28th. Or after lunch.

It's slow, it's brittle, and it gets worse as transaction volume rises. One typo or timing error and the whole balance sheet is suspect. Every mismatch is a time sink. Every fix comes with a double-check.

AI is pulling that work forward and turning it into a background process.

BlackLine, a leading financial automation platform, uses machine learning to match transactions across bank statements, ERP systems, and subledgers. Its auto-certification engine can now resolve over 85% of standard reconciliations without human review.

That doesn't mean it's locked. It means the system flags only the edge cases. Accountants go straight to what needs judgment. The rest disappears into throughput.

That's how time compounding begins—by skipping the first round of tedium and starting deeper in the stack.

FloQast, built by CPAs, targets the close process directly. Its AI prioritizes incomplete entries, highlights inconsistencies, and suggests resolution steps based on prior months' data. Mid-sized firms say it's shaved two to three days off the monthly close. Over a year, that's more than a month of regained operating capacity.

That time doesn't just vanish. It gets redirected to analysis, scenario modeling, and tax planning. The work shifts up the value chain.

Vic.ai, aimed at accounts payable, uses AI to extract, classify, and approve invoices in real time. One construction company running high-volume vendor transactions reduced invoice processing time by 80%. AP staff didn't get laid off. They got reassigned to vendor negotiations and payment strategy.

When the bottom layer of approval work gets compressed, the next layer of value shows up.

Even QuickBooks now includes predictive categorizations based on past behavior. What used to require ten clicks becomes one. That's small in isolation. But when you're tagging thousands of transactions, it adds up fast.

Time doesn't just get saved. It gets rerouted.

Corporate controllers are using MindBridge to scan general ledgers for anomalies. The AI applies statistical and behavioral analytics to spot errors, fraud risk, and outlier trends. It's not just matching rows. It's questioning logic.

That used to be the job of a forensic accountant. Now it runs continuously, flagging only what breaks expectation.

When you know where to look, you stop wasting time checking everything.

At a regional accounting firm in Ohio, the partners integrated a GPT-based assistant trained on their SOPs. It generates draft emails for client follow-ups, suggests phrasing for audit findings, and populates engagement letters with custom fee language.

It's not perfect. But it gets them 70% of the way to a polished product. That's an hour saved per day, per partner. Multiply that by 12 partners and 50 weeks, and the capacity gain speaks for itself.

None of this automates the audit. But it does automate the friction around it.

AI is doing to accounting what macros did to Excel—only smarter, and with memory.

The job hasn't changed. It still requires precision, standards, and judgment. But the entry point has shifted. Accountants now start with organized inputs and fewer distractions. That compounds over time—not just into faster closes, but into quieter months, better forecasting, and more retained staff.

AI doesn't fix accounting. It just keeps the busywork from stealing the whole day.

And that alone changes the tempo of a firm.

20

AUDITORS: RISK-BASED SAMPLING AT SCALE

Traditional audits depend on sampling. Pick a few transactions, check the math, write up the findings. If nothing stands out, sign off.

But that model was built for paper. In a digital ledger world, it's slow, partial, and increasingly out of step with the volume and velocity of modern finance.

AI isn't making audits obsolete. It's just shifting the unit of work—from sampling to screening, from spot checks to systems.

MindBridge, one of the leaders in AI auditing, uses a hybrid statistical-behavioral model to run anomaly detection on entire general ledgers. It evaluates risk on every transaction, based on both magnitude and behavior. It doesn't replace the auditor. It replaces the random walk.

The auditor doesn't pick samples anymore. The AI picks patterns.

Firms using MindBridge have reported that upwards of 90% of audit prep time now goes into interpreting findings—not locating them. That's the definition of time compounding: start where the value begins, not where the data sits.

PwC launched their proprietary Halo platform to pull similar functions into their own process. It ingests full transactional data sets and looks for red flags: unexpected relationships, timing gaps, duplicate vendors, missing authorizations. One of their use cases involved a client with 500,000 transactions. Halo flagged 38 that triggered multi-factor anomalies.

The auditor didn't just find errors. They found blind spots in controls—before regulators did.

At Deloitte, their Argus platform integrates natural language models to assist in document-intensive audits. Instead of flipping through PDF contracts, the system extracts lease terms, triggers, and revenue recognition notes. Audit teams validate, not compile. The clock starts later. The review goes deeper.

Smaller firms are gaining leverage too. CaseWare, a provider of cloud-based audit solutions, offers AI-powered working paper prep and documentation checks. It identifies inconsistencies between financial statements and supporting schedules. For firms with lean teams, this saves hours per engagement—time that would've gone into double-checking footnotes and cross-referencing tick marks.

The common thread isn't automation. It's pre-processing. AI creates a jump point. What used to require 12 hours of baseline work gets boiled down to two, with better visibility.

That shift changes how risk is assessed. Auditors no longer rely on historical assumptions. They move based on real-time signals.

It also changes when client conversations happen. One mid-sized firm using AI tools now holds risk review meetings in week two, not week five. Early pattern recognition means early intervention. And clients respond better to flags raised proactively than to findings buried in a final report.

This doesn't just save time. It makes the audit collaborative again.

On the backend, AI is also helping teams close files faster. Tools like Validis and Inflo automate client data ingestion and formatting. The files arrive clean, with mappings already aligned to the audit platform. Staff don't spend time formatting CSVs. They spend time analyzing risk.

In aggregate, these tools don't make audits shorter. They make the early steps faster, so the later steps get more attention. That shift shows up in retention, because junior staff aren't stuck doing cleanup for six weeks straight.

Auditing isn't disappearing. It's just finally catching up to the speed of the business it monitors.

AI in audit compresses the low-value tasks and extends the runway for high-value analysis. The client gets a tighter report. The team gets a clearer workload. And the firm gets faster cycles with fewer surprises.

That's how time compounds in audit—not by skipping steps, but by starting at the part that actually needs judgment.

21

MANUFACTURING: AI-DRIVEN QUALITY AND DOWNTIME PREDICTION

In manufacturing, lost time isn't abstract. It shows up as idle machines, missed quotas, or defect recalls. Every delay or defect costs money—and worse, trust.

AI isn't transforming manufacturing with theory. It's doing it with sensors, schedules, and pattern detection.

Siemens uses predictive maintenance powered by machine learning in its gas turbine division. The system tracks temperature, vibration, and load data in real time. When anomalies appear—changes in acoustic profiles, micro-variations in output—the system recommends preemptive service.

That reduces unplanned downtime by over 30%. It also changes how teams think about scheduling. Maintenance shifts from reactive to routed. The result isn't just fewer breakdowns. It's steadier throughput.

Time that used to be lost to emergencies now gets budgeted like inventory.

Fanuc, a Japanese robotics firm, embeds AI directly into its CNC systems. Their FIELD system tracks machine cycles and compares performance across similar units. When cycle times drift or error rates rise, the system flags it. Operators adjust before product quality slips.

Factories using FIELD have reported up to a 15% improvement in OEE—overall equipment effectiveness. That doesn't happen from faster robots. It happens from faster feedback.

Quality control is seeing the same shift.

Landing AI, an image recognition startup spun out by Andrew Ng, offers defect detection for assembly lines. You don't need thousands of images to train it. A few dozen will do. Their platform uses small data to build flexible models, ideal for low-volume, high-precision manufacturing.

A midwestern auto parts supplier using Landing AI flagged 42% more defects in the first month after deployment—without hiring new QA staff.

Time wasn't saved on the inspection. It was saved on the rework.

At Bosch, engineers use AI to predict which components will fail inspection before the process is complete. The algorithm pulls sensor data mid-process and assigns a failure probability. If the threshold crosses a certain line, the system adjusts on the fly—slowing the line, increasing precision, or diverting to a secondary path.

That's not just quality assurance. That's real-time process control.

And it reduces wasted motion, which is where manufacturing time tends to die quietly.

Predictive maintenance is scaling across sectors. General Motors uses AI to monitor paint booth operations. Airflow, humidity, and chemical mix all factor in. When the model predicts a future defect cluster, it adjusts airflow settings automatically. That keeps the line running and avoids batch waste.

The paint line doesn't shut down. The audit never happens. The scrap pile stays empty.

That's how AI compounds time in manufacturing. Not with speedups, but with fewer slowdowns.

The same logic applies to supply chain forecasting. Flex, a global manufacturer, uses AI to model inventory positions across suppliers and factories. Instead of monthly adjustments, their system runs daily simulations. If a supplier misses a delivery, the model flags downstream impacts.

They've reduced excess inventory by over 15%, while improving fulfillment. That's not optimization. That's time redistribution at the logistical level.

On the floor, it's simpler. Less waiting. Fewer surprises. Smoother shifts.

Operators aren't being replaced. They're being given foresight. They're starting each day closer to resolution.

That's what AI delivers here—not perfection, but rhythm.

And when the line stays in rhythm, everything else gets easier.

22

CONSTRUCTION: SCHEDULING, PERMITS, AND SITE MONITORING

Construction runs on sequence. When one task stalls, everything stacks up behind it.

Delays cost more than money—they ripple through materials, crews, inspections, and liability. Everyone's waiting on someone else. That's the margin AI is starting to unlock.

OpenSpace, a construction-focused AI platform, uses computer vision to track job site progress. A field worker straps on a helmet-mounted camera, walks the site, and uploads the footage. The AI compares the visual data to project blueprints and schedules. It highlights what's ahead, what's behind, and what's off-plan.

Firms using OpenSpace report up to 40% reductions in status-check walk-throughs. Project managers get automatic progress reports without chasing down subcontractors. Coordination improves. Meetings get shorter.

That's how time compounds in construction—by compressing the feedback loop.

Permitting is also shifting. In Dubai, the city's Building Permit system now uses AI to pre-screen building applications for code violations. The AI checks zoning, occupancy, fire regulations, and structural limits. If there's a conflict, the system flags it instantly.

Architects and contractors no longer wait two weeks to learn something's wrong. They learn on submission.

It doesn't just speed up approvals. It reduces rework.

For job site safety, Smartvid.io offers an AI platform called Vinnie that scans site photos and video for violations—missing PPE, blocked exits, trip hazards. The system doesn't just issue alerts. It tracks safety metrics by crew and subcontractor.

Companies using it have seen reductions in lost-time incidents and insurance claims. But they've also seen fewer schedule slowdowns. When safety improves, inspections go faster. Fewer citations mean fewer pauses.

These are not marginal gains. They accumulate.

Procore, already dominant in construction project management, has started layering in AI to suggest task reprioritization. If concrete is delayed and steel is early, the system recommends reshuffling crews. What used to be a three-call negotiation becomes a button.

That's hours saved every week—across hundreds of projects.

Doxel, another AI-driven site platform, uses lidar and 360-degree cameras to build 3D maps of job sites. It tracks productivity against planned budgets and timelines. If framing takes longer than expected, the system flags it the next day—not two weeks later.

The data drives early corrections. Superintendents stay proactive instead of reactive. Small delays stop becoming big ones.

One of the more subtle shifts comes in document management. Construction generates endless PDFs—RFIs, submittals, inspection forms. Buildots, an AI tool for document control, classifies and links these documents to specific site areas and phases. That cuts search time down dramatically.

Less time spent tracking paperwork means more time on actual construction.

Some developers are using AI to evaluate subcontractor bids. They scan prior job performance, average delay time, change order frequency, and pricing variance. Instead of just picking the lowest number, GCs now pick the most stable outcome.

That reduces mid-project contractor turnover, which is one of the biggest hidden time sinks in the industry.

These tools don't build walls or pour foundations. But they restore flow. They compress the slack between trades and the gaps between updates. And over a 14-month timeline, that turns into weeks.

AI isn't changing the tools. It's changing the tempo.

And in construction, that's everything.

23

RETAIL: DYNAMIC PRICING, INVENTORY, AND STAFFING

Retail runs on thin margins and tight cycles. If pricing lags, inventory bloats. If staffing misses, conversion drops. The timing is unforgiving.

AI is helping retailers close the gaps—by accelerating decisions that used to rely on last week's numbers.

Walmart uses AI to optimize shelf restocking and inventory visibility. Its Intelligent Retail Lab pilot store in Levittown, New York, deployed real-time shelf monitoring through computer vision. Cameras and sensors feed into a backend system that flags low stock, misplaced items, and product gaps.

What used to be a visual check is now a rolling alert. That reduces the time between depletion and replenishment. It also shortens the window where customers walk away because something isn't there.

That's not just automation. That's reclaiming missed sales.

In pricing, companies like Kroger use dynamic pricing systems trained on competitor data, loyalty trends, and local weather. The system adjusts prices daily, sometimes hourly. If a heatwave hits, bottled water doesn't just move—it's repriced instantly.

The result isn't gouging. It's flow. Overstock disappears faster. Promotions target the moment, not the month.

Time compounds here by preventing slow stock turnover—and dead inventory that eats margins later.

Zara, part of Inditex, integrates AI into inventory allocation. It predicts what stores will need, not just based on past sales, but on real-time demand signals—returns, web traffic, regional trends. This lets them ship shorter, faster runs of clothing and avoid long markdown windows.

Their sell-through rate is higher than peers, because they don't overbuild inventory they'll have to discount.

The real savings come not from one prediction, but from dozens made daily that keep product closer to demand.

Staffing is getting the same treatment. Gap Inc. uses AI to forecast labor needs in real time. The system factors in weather, local events, foot traffic, and sales trends. Shifts adjust dynamically—not just week to week, but day to day.

That changes how managers build schedules. It also cuts down on overstaffing and burnout. If two associates can handle Tuesday morning, why pay four?

Every shift that runs lean but covers demand is a direct margin gain.

Even planogram compliance is speeding up. Shelf-Engine, used in grocery, automates order decisions based on sales velocity and shrinkage. When yogurt sits too long or bananas brown too fast, the system dials back the next order.

That reduces spoilage and restocking costs. But it also gives back the buyer's time. Instead of reviewing every SKU, they only review exceptions.

That's the pattern in modern retail AI: let the system handle the 80%, and free up the human for the 20% that moves the needle.

Some companies are layering AI into training. Lowe's piloted an in-store mobile assistant that answers employee questions about inventory locations, restocking, and policy. That reduces onboarding time and gets new hires customer-ready faster.

It also keeps seasoned staff from wasting time answering the same procedural questions over and over.

The effect isn't visible on a chart, but it compounds in the background—fewer delays, shorter wait times, smoother shifts.

None of these tools are particularly glamorous. They run quiet. They don't pitch new strategies. They make the old ones run faster, cheaper, tighter.

That's the edge in retail now. Not more data. Faster action.

And in a business where timing decides margin, that speed adds up quickly.

24

TRANSPORTATION: ROUTING, DISPATCH, AND MAINTENANCE

In transportation, small delays become big costs. Ten extra minutes at scale can sink a week's margin. AI is tightening those windows—one route, one dispatch, one engine at a time.

UPS uses AI to refine route optimization through its ORION platform. It doesn't just plot delivery paths. It adjusts them in real time based on traffic, package volume, and driver behavior. The system saved the company 10 million gallons of fuel in a single year and cut over 100 million miles from its routes.

But the deeper gain isn't mileage. It's predictability.

The route runs tighter. The schedule stops slipping. And that compounds across every driver, every day.

In public transit, the city of Pittsburgh tested AI traffic signal optimization with a system called Surtrac. The system adjusted light timing dynamically based on vehicle flow, reducing travel time by over 25% and intersection wait times by 40%.

That's not just better traffic. That's smoother bus routes and tighter dispatch windows—without adding a single lane.

AI compresses the time vehicles spend idle, waiting on a system built for averages. It turns the network from fixed to adaptive.

In freight, Convoy—a digital freight network—uses AI to match shippers and carriers with real-time pricing and load optimization. When a truck finishes a delivery, Convoy already knows where the next best load is. Deadhead miles drop. Truck utilization rises.

That saves fuel, but more importantly, it saves planning time. The driver moves. The dispatcher watches the board, not the phone.

Fleet maintenance is also shifting.

Ryder uses predictive analytics across its rental fleet to anticipate vehicle failure before it happens. Oil temperature, brake wear, tire pressure—everything feeds into a model that flags issues days in advance. Instead of breakdowns, Ryder schedules service proactively.

Downtime doesn't just shrink. It gets built into the calendar.

Smaller operators are catching up. Samsara offers AI-powered dash cams that analyze driver behavior—hard stops, distracted driving, harsh turns. Fleet managers use this to coach drivers, reduce risk, and flag vehicles for preventative checks based on real-world strain.

Time is saved not by removing risk, but by moving the review cycle earlier.

School bus fleets are also going digital. Zūm, an AI-powered student transportation startup, optimizes routes daily based on student absences, traffic, and driver availability. It updates in real time and auto-notifies parents.

The result? Fewer late arrivals. Fewer phone calls. More trust.

Even long-haul rail is integrating AI. Canadian National Railway uses predictive maintenance and scheduling tools to monitor freight car condition and optimize routing. When you run thousands of miles of track, small efficiency gains become quarter-long improvements.

That's the real pattern here. AI doesn't always shave hours. But it shaves minutes in 10,000 places. That's how transportation wins.

Dispatchers spend less time rerouting. Mechanics fix before failures. Drivers hit tighter windows with less uncertainty.

The effect compounds because the system stops waiting on lag.

AI isn't changing the vehicle. It's changing the cadence.

And when the whole network moves in rhythm, the gains start to feel exponential.

25

REAL ESTATE: UNDERWRITING, LISTINGS, AND LEAD ROUTING

Real estate is a timing game. Speed determines who gets the listing, who closes the buyer, and who wins the offer. The faster agent, lender, or investor usually wins.

AI is making the gap wider.

Redfin uses AI to value homes based on thousands of real-time market signals—recent sales, local trends, renovation data, and seasonality. Its algorithm adjusts prices nightly. Sellers get data-informed recommendations without waiting on a full CMA.

That doesn't replace the agent. It compresses the prep. Instead of a two-hour comp session, they walk into the listing appointment with the number already scoped.

That speeds up the pitch. And time is leverage in front of a seller.

Zillow's Premier Agent program uses AI to route buyer inquiries to agents most likely to respond quickly and convert. It doesn't just hand leads out in a round-robin. It optimizes for close probability, based on past response times, deal flow, and communication style.

The agent who responds fastest gets more leads. That creates a feedback loop that compounds. Fast becomes faster.

Opendoor uses machine learning to underwrite homes in under 24 hours. Its models evaluate property condition, local price velocity, and repair costs to generate instant offers. Sellers who opt in skip staging, showings, and weekends of uncertainty.

Behind the scenes, the underwriting team gets an AI-generated property profile—flagging outliers and recommending price adjustments. That collapses what used to take three departments into one workflow.

Time saved on underwriting turns into more deals closed before competitors even call.

In commercial real estate, REoptimizer uses AI to evaluate tenant needs against thousands of available lease options. It identifies mismatches in square footage, amenities, and cost projections—before the first tour is even booked.

Brokers save time by not showing the wrong space. Tenants save time by seeing only what fits.

On the investor side, Localize is using AI to filter and score residential listings based on user behavior. It tracks what buyers browse, what they save, and how long they linger. That data feeds into a recommendation engine that emails listings likely to convert.

Agents using Localize say their average time-to-response is shorter, and their conversion-to-tour ratio is tighter. They don't just send more listings. They send better ones.

In mortgage, Blend automates loan pre-approval using customer data and third-party verifications. Borrowers upload pay stubs. The system pulls tax data, bank records, and employment history behind the scenes. Pre-approval letters arrive in minutes.

Lenders using Blend shave days off their pipeline. They also reduce dropoff. The faster the approval lands, the fewer borrowers walk away.

Time compounding shows up everywhere here—not in huge savings, but in small deltas that add up.

Agents get to the seller first. Lenders approve before the buyer gets cold feet. Platforms keep leads in the right lanes. No single step is miraculous. But every one is a little faster. And that makes the whole machine leaner.

AI isn't transforming real estate strategy. It's transforming the clock it runs on.

And in this business, the clock is the market.

26

ARCHITECTURE AND DESIGN: GENERATIVE LAYOUTS AND CLIENT CUSTOMIZATION

Architects don't lack ideas. They lack time to test them.

Design is iterative. Every layout is a trade-off—light versus cost, flow versus code, form versus budget. What slows the process isn't creativity. It's constraints.

AI is now generating faster paths through those constraints.

TestFit is a generative design platform used in urban planning and multifamily development. You feed it a site plan, zoning rules, parking minimums, and unit mix. In under a minute, it produces optimized layout options. Floor plates, parking ratios, cost estimates—it's all there.

That used to take a team a full day. Now it happens while you sip coffee.

And if the client says, "What if we flip the entry?" the model adjusts on the fly. That's time compounding in real form: fewer hours spent rebuilding, more hours spent refining.

In New York, the firm SHoP Architects has integrated AI tools to generate façade concepts based on historical data and solar exposure. Instead of sketching ten options, the system generates hundreds. The architect doesn't pick the best. They pick the starting point.

Designers still decide. AI just gets them past blank screens faster.

Zaha Hadid Architects uses machine learning to evaluate structural stress during concept design. Instead of waiting on engineering input, they surface structural constraints early. The back-and-forth gets shorter. The guesswork shrinks.

This isn't automation. It's alignment. Engineers, architects, and planners now start closer together.

In interior design, Modsy and DecorMatters use AI to generate room mockups based on photos and style preferences. Homeowners drag in furniture. The system adjusts dimensions, color palettes, and layout recommendations in real time.

Designers use this to speed up approvals. What used to take a week of back-and-forth gets locked in on a call.

Some firms are going further. Autodesk's Project Refinery lets architects optimize designs for daylight, HVAC load, and embodied carbon—all before construction begins. Instead of simulating one option at a time, they simulate thousands. The best versions surface automatically.

The time savings aren't in the sketch. They're in not having to redo the sketch three weeks later.

Even code compliance is getting pulled forward. UpCodes uses natural language models to analyze local building code and flag violations in design documents. It doesn't approve plans. It helps architects avoid known pitfalls before submittal.

Firms using UpCodes reduce code-related plan revisions by up to 40%. That's not just fewer errors. That's weeks off the review cycle.

AI is also showing up in client presentations. Tools like ArkDesign use generative models to turn zoning inputs into marketing-ready visuals. The architect doesn't spend three days building a presentation deck. They spend one hour editing what AI made.

It's not about skipping the process. It's about starting ahead of where they used to start.

Architects still own the taste. They still make the calls. But now, they arrive at those decisions with more clarity and fewer iterations.

That's how time compounds in design—less redraw, more resolve.

AI doesn't change the architect. It changes how long it takes to become one on a given project.

27

FILM, TV, AND VIDEO: SCRIPTS, EDITS, AND PRODUCTION TIMELINES

Film and video production isn't slow because people are inefficient. It's slow because creative decisions live inside nonlinear workflows. Scripts don't turn into dailies. They move through outlines, treatments, budgets, boards, crews, cameras, and software. Time disappears in the transitions.

AI is helping compress that timeline by moving work forward before it gets handed off.

In scripting, tools like Jasper and Sudowrite assist with first-pass screenplays. Writers input beats, tone, and character direction. The model generates a working draft in seconds. It's not ready to shoot. But it's faster than outlining from scratch, especially when the goal is getting to a usable structure quickly.

Time compounds here because the writer doesn't burn two days on a false start. They see the structure. They move.

Storyboarding is speeding up too. Runway, Pika Labs, and Kaiber AI can generate visual scenes from text prompts. Directors use them to sketch mood, blocking, and transitions before committing resources. This isn't final artwork. It's directional framing. But it prevents crews from walking onto set without alignment.

Every decision made before the scout saves money. But it also saves time in morale, confusion, and rework.

Editing is where time really adds up. Adobe Premiere Pro now allows timeline edits through its transcript view. Editors can remove lines from a documentary or promo by deleting the corresponding text. It reduces cutdown work from 45 minutes to 10.

Descript does the same for podcast video. You import the file. It transcribes, identifies speakers, removes filler words, and exports a cleaner cut—all before you've touched a blade tool.

Time used to vanish in the scrub. Now it gets spent refining intent.

DaVinci Resolve's machine learning models suggest initial color corrections based on prior footage. This gets colorists closer to parity across shots without building every grade from scratch. It's not creative direction—it's a head start.

Sound design is also being compressed. Adobe's Speech Enhance tool uses AI to clean up low-quality audio. It removes reverb, boosts clarity, and normalizes levels. It can't fix a bad mic, but it can prevent a reshoot.

What used to be an emergency becomes a solved task.

Preproduction planning benefits from AI as well. StudioBinder now layers scene complexity into its call sheet scheduling tools. The system evaluates estimated shot duration, crew fatigue, and location logistics to flag vulnerable sequences. Assistant directors don't rebuild the plan every night. They refine it.

One skipped delay saves thousands. But even small nudges—five minutes gained per scene—stack across a month-long shoot.

Post is increasingly structured for output variation. Runway's Gen-2 model and Pictory.ai enable automatic reformatting of horizontal edits into TikTok, Reels, and Shorts. Editors don't rebuild. They export alternate cuts. Captions, pacing, and aspect ratios adjust on the fly.

That turns a single deliverable into five without extending the deadline.

Licensing is getting automated as well. Rightsline and FilmTrack use AI to check licensing metadata against regional rules, expiration dates, and prior usages. Distributors know where a track or clip can be used without legal re-review. This saves lawyers' time, but also avoids last-minute scrubs before release.

And in casting, a few platforms now allow bulk audition review by tagging performance traits—vocal tone, timing, physicality—and sorting by fit. The casting director still chooses. But they see the best five options early, not after 200 clips.

The gain isn't in skipping judgment. It's in skipping the search for signal.

AI won't write a story, light a set, or direct a performance. But it eliminates the guesswork in how all those things fit together. It compresses the structure around creativity.

And that's where time multiplies—not by reducing the work, but by reducing the orbit around the work.

28

MUSIC: COMPOSITION, LICENSING, AND DISTRIBUTION

Music production doesn't stall at the piano. It stalls in versioning, approvals, stems, sync, and metadata. The bottleneck isn't always the melody. It's everything orbiting the track.

AI is now moving music faster—through composition, licensing, and delivery—without replacing the creative core.

Endlesss, an AI-assisted collaborative platform, lets musicians loop, layer, and build compositions live across devices. It handles syncing, leveling, and session recall. Artists don't wait to bounce stems or render exports. They just play. The system tracks it all.

The time saved isn't in writing. It's in not having to stop.

Amper Music and Aiva generate royalty-free compositions for background use—podcasts, YouTube, ads. You pick tempo, instrumentation, mood. The AI produces full-length tracks in under two minutes. Creators edit structure and export stems directly.

Instead of paying for custom scoring or navigating royalty licensing, users get tracks that are legally clean and structurally flexible.

That's time saved in both legal review and creative delay.

In professional studios, LANDR automates mastering. Engineers upload a mix. The AI applies EQ curves, compression profiles, and volume balancing based on genre and reference tracks. It's not replacing a trained ear, but it produces a solid draft master in under five minutes.

That compresses the back-and-forth between producer and engineer. And it gives independents a way to stay in the release cycle without waiting on studio time.

For vocal production, tools like Lalal.ai isolate or remove vocals and instruments from existing tracks. Producers can sample or remix without re-recording. That's time recovered from licensing negotiations—or from recreating something that already exists.

Descript's Overdub feature allows creators to generate voiceovers with AI clones of their own voice. Musicians and podcasters use it to fix ad tags, intros, or liner notes without reopening the mic. A three-word correction happens in a few keystrokes.

The time cost of small mistakes drops to near zero.

Licensing and sync are also shifting.

SyncFloor and Songtradr use AI to match songs to commercial briefs. A brand wants "cinematic, female vocal, mid-tempo, with a hopeful tone." The engine returns results with pre-cleared rights, duration matches, and pricing.

Music supervisors don't wade through folders or ping rights holders. They select, drag, and deal.

This turns what used to be a four-week sync search into a one-hour task. It also pulls independent musicians into licensing ecosystems that were once gated by catalogs and reps.

On the distribution side, DistroKid uses automated formatting and metadata verification to reduce rejections by streaming services. The system checks ISRC codes, normalizes track volume, and flags duplicates before submission.

That prevents the invisible two-day delay that comes from an upload error. The artist never sees the problem because it never gets submitted wrong in the first place.

Even royalties are getting compressed. Stem automates payout splits between collaborators. Revenue goes directly to the producer, writer, and featured artist based on preset percentages. No spreadsheets. No monthly disputes.

That doesn't just save emails. It protects relationships—and those relationships are the engine of fast creative cycles.

Music hasn't gotten easier to make. But the work around it—the admin, the export, the rights—has gotten faster. And that's where AI is having real impact.

It's not rewriting the hook. It's removing the drag.

And when artists stop waiting for a reply, a render, or a signature, they don't just produce more. They move forward.

That's time compounding in the music business. Not in the session. In everything that surrounds it.

* Chapter 23: Traders – Signal Extraction and Portfolio Rebalancing

Speed used to be a trading edge. Now, it's table stakes.

AI isn't just helping traders move faster. It's changing what they look at, how signals emerge, and when rebalancing decisions get triggered.

Citadel and Two Sigma use machine learning models to detect nonlinear relationships between macro indicators and asset prices. These aren't just regression models. They identify conditions where signals emerge only under certain volatility, rate, or correlation regimes. That changes the entire shape of what's tradable.

Traders stop scanning the surface. They start drilling contextually—when GDP surprises matter, when liquidity dries up, when yield curves invert *and* tech earnings slip.

The model doesn't replace judgment. It reorders where the judgment starts.

Retail platforms are integrating similar intelligence. Robinhood and eToro now surface anomaly detection and option flow indicators previously reserved for institutional desks. Traders see where volume is outsized, or sentiment diverges, without needing to code a screen.

This doesn't just save minutes. It compresses learning curves by months.

AI also powers rebalancing decisions. Wealthfront uses AI to monitor drift across customer portfolios. When allocations stray from targets, it executes partial trades using tax-loss harvesting algorithms and risk-tolerance settings. The entire process is invisible to the user.

Behind the scenes, rebalancing used to require weekly batch runs. Now it's continuous.

And that compounds time. Drifts don't fester. Clients stay aligned. The machine doesn't wait for human lag.

In crypto, platforms like Numerai and dYdX use decentralized AI models that blend crowd-submitted strategies into a meta-model. Traders contribute signals. The system weights them by performance and stability. What used to take a fund six months of backtesting gets simulated and scored overnight.

The edge here isn't who built the strategy—it's who deploys it into the faster loop.

Hedge funds are automating research signals from alt data. JP Morgan's LOXM trading engine incorporates satellite imagery, earnings call transcripts, and social sentiment into pre-trade analysis. The signals are soft, but the aggregation gives shape to macro themes earlier than traditional filters.

When five weak signals converge, they move before the headline does.

This doesn't remove the trader. It removes the delay between market noise and structured conviction.

Execution is also changing. Smart order routing now uses reinforcement learning. Tools from firms like Clearpool and Exegy adjust execution paths in real time based on venue speed, fill rates, and microstructure dynamics.

A human couldn't keep up. AI doesn't need to pause.

These aren't just tools. They're system changes. They shift how often trades get reevaluated, how rapidly ideas cycle, and how much dead capital sits unallocated.

Time compounds here not in the strategy, but in everything around it.

Fewer clicks. Fewer stale signals. Fewer hours wasted reading after the move already happened.

The market still punishes slow. But now, slow doesn't mean late. It means linear.

And in an adaptive system, that's fatal.

PART III

A DAY IN THE LIFE (WITH AI)

29

ASSOCIATION CONFERENCE
MANAGER

7:00 AM. The manager arrives on site. Before the coffee's even brewed, she reviews overnight emails with Microsoft Copilot or Gmail's AI summaries. The tool clusters vendor questions, speaker updates, and attendee issues. Urgent tasks are flagged, and low-priority notes are suggested for auto-reply. Inbox triage is handled before the team walk-through begins.

7:30 AM. Schedule check. Instead of scrolling through spreadsheets, the manager opens her Whova or Cvent dashboard—platforms with built-in AI agenda optimization. The system highlights overlapping sessions, speaker conflicts, and real-time room utilization. Suggestions for smoothing out traffic flows and session timing land instantly, saving hours of manual slotting.

8:00 AM. Vendor coordination. ChatGPT drafts concise update texts to caterers, AV, and hotel staff. For vendors who don't reply, the system suggests reminder scripts. Contracts and schedules are uploaded into Lexion or Ironclad (AI-powered contract management), which flags expiring terms, missing signatures, and payment deadlines. Instead of "chasing paper," the manager moves straight to problem-solving.

9:00 AM. Attendee check-in. Registration is run by a platform like Eventbrite or Swoogo, which now offer facial recognition or QR code-based AI check-in. The system flags VIPs, alerts staff to special needs, and tracks real-time headcounts. Late arrivals receive auto-generated SMS reminders with their schedule and directions.

10:00 AM. Speaker wrangling. Using a Slack channel or SMS bot, the manager pushes automated reminders and room assignments to each speaker. ChatGPT is used to draft "thank you" notes or emergency schedule changes. If a speaker cancels, the AI scans for backup presenters with similar topics or credentials and suggests outreach instantly.

11:00 AM. Social media monitoring. Sprout Social or Hootsuite's AI modules summarize attendee tweets and posts. The manager gets a dashboard of trending topics, complaints, and highlights—plus suggested responses for both praise and issues. Instead of manually monitoring five platforms, she responds in a unified flow.

12:00 PM. Lunch logistics. The manager uses Otter.ai to record team debriefs and feedback. The tool transcribes, tags action items, and syncs follow-ups to her project management board (Asana or Trello, both with AI plugins). Vendor invoices are checked by QuickBooks AI, which flags payment anomalies and pending approvals.

1:00 PM. Session monitoring. The conference app collects real-time attendee feedback using AI sentiment analysis. If session ratings dip, the system alerts the manager and suggests "room drop-ins" to check on A/V or speaker pacing. Attendee questions submitted through the app are clustered by topic, making panel Q&A sessions more focused and efficient.

2:00 PM. Networking. ChatGPT drafts personalized introductions for VIPs, sponsors, and speakers based on LinkedIn bios and registration data. These are sent as text or app messages to help guests make meaningful connections—no awkward icebreakers or missed opportunities.

3:00 PM. Crisis averted. A weather alert threatens a scheduled outdoor reception. The manager asks ChatGPT to generate a relocation plan, complete with sample attendee messages and updated signage copy. Event diagrams are updated using Canva's Magic Design, saving hours of graphic prep.

4:00 PM. Final checks. All contracts, expenses, and feedback are summarized by AI tools for end-of-day reporting. Action items for tomorrow are generated and emailed to the team automatically. The manager reviews only the exceptions.

5:00 PM. Debrief. A brief AI-generated report summarizes attendance, top-rated sessions, vendor performance, and immediate issues. The manager edits for nuance and sends it to association leadership.

By compressing each workflow loop—email, schedule, vendor, attendee, reporting—the manager spends less time in crisis and more time making the meeting run.

AI won't solve every problem. But now, the biggest drag on conference management isn't time. It's just what happens when real people gather.

30

CAR SALESMAN

8:00 AM. The salesman starts the day with a quick review of new leads. Instead of manual spreadsheet work, he uses ChatGPT or Google Gemini (via the web app or mobile) to summarize overnight website inquiries and social media messages. He pastes emails into the AI tool and asks for a prioritized list based on purchase intent, follow-up urgency, and any prior communications. In fifteen minutes, he's got a call sheet, sorted by opportunity.

9:00 AM. Preparing for walk-ins. The salesman checks his personal notes and CRM for appointments. For new prospects, he pastes customer names into LinkedIn or Facebook, then uses an AI tool to draft a brief background or suggest talking points based on publicly visible info. This makes his initial conversations more focused—no time wasted on "discovery" for the basics.

10:00 AM. Digital marketing outreach. Between appointments, he uses Canva's Magic Write (or ChatGPT with a prompt) to generate personalized email templates for following up on unsold prospects from last week. He asks AI to draft three versions: one for SUV shoppers, one for used-car buyers, and one for those seeking financing. The emails are ready to send in minutes, with content more specific than generic dealership blasts.

11:00 AM. Inventory questions. A customer calls about vehicle availability. Instead of hunting through the dealership site or calling the back office, the salesman uses a browser plugin (like Perplexity or ChatGPT Advanced Data Analysis) to quickly search and summarize the current inventory list. He copies a filtered, AI-generated summary into a text to the customer, saving time and presenting as "always on."

12:00 PM. Lunch break—content creation. The salesman uses an AI video tool (InVideo, Synthesia, or even TikTok's AI editing) to record a short "walkaround" of a new arrival on the lot. The AI suggests edits, adds captions, and polishes the clip for social media. Instead of outsourcing to the marketing department, he posts content directly, engaging buyers faster.

1:00 PM. Handling customer objections. During an in-person meeting, the customer asks a technical question about hybrid warranties. The salesman types the question into ChatGPT on his phone for a clear, jargon-free answer. He relays the facts instantly, building trust and keeping the conversation moving.

2:00 PM. Test drive paperwork. The salesman uploads a scanned license photo into a mobile OCR app (Adobe Scan, Microsoft Lens) that extracts details and fills out the test drive form digitally. No paper forms, no redundant typing. He texts the customer a digital copy and logs it for compliance.

3:00 PM. Trade-in research. A customer is curious about their car's value. The salesman uses Carvana or Kelley Blue Book's online estimator, but if the customer is hesitant, he feeds the VIN, mileage, and condition details into ChatGPT and asks it to summarize trade-in pros/cons and provide a concise, persuasive rationale for the offer.

4:00 PM. Financing and forms. The salesman helps the customer fill out an online loan pre-qualification. If there's confusion about any terms, he enters the legalese into ChatGPT and gets a simple explanation to share with the buyer. This eliminates confusion and keeps the deal moving forward.

5:00 PM. End-of-day follow-up. The salesman summarizes key interactions by dictating voice notes into Otter.ai, which transcribes and organizes them for CRM entry or team sharing. AI-generated to-do lists for tomorrow's leads, test drives, and follow-ups are ready in minutes.

AI isn't running the sales floor. But it is cutting hours of admin, communication, and prep. Every tool in this workflow is real, personal, and ready to use right now.

And in sales, the time you don't waste is time you can spend closing.

31

CEO'S ASSISTANT AT A HOSPITAL

7:00 AM. The assistant arrives before the hospital stirs. First task: review the CEO's inbox. Traditionally, this would mean scanning hundreds of emails, flagging urgent requests, and building a hand-curated priority list. Now, an AI email triage tool (like Microsoft 365 Copilot) scans the night's messages, summarizing threads, auto-prioritizing based on sender and keyword, and suggesting replies for low-urgency items. In fifteen minutes, the assistant clears what used to take forty.

7:45 AM. Calendar chaos. The CEO's day is filled with back-to-back meetings: physician groups, finance, board prep, and unexpected drop-ins. AI calendar assistants (Clara, x.ai, or even Google's built-in scheduling) propose slot swaps, room changes, and consolidate travel buffers. The tool auto-reschedules when clinics overrun or emergencies pop up. Instead of a game of Tetris, the calendar flows.

8:30 AM. Document prep. There's a meeting with the board at 10:00. Instead of pulling old slides, drafting new talking points, and hunting through spreadsheets, the assistant uses a generative document tool. It digests last quarter's board minutes, finds updated financials, and produces a summary slide deck. The assistant checks for accuracy, tweaks tone, and prints—shaving two hours of document wrangling down to forty minutes.

9:30 AM. The CEO's rounds begin. The assistant tracks location using an internal AI-powered locator (like an enhanced version of Stanley Healthcare's platform), updating the calendar dynamically if the CEO is delayed by a patient visit or ER issue. Meanwhile, messages from clinicians are parsed by a chatbot, which drafts responses for routine questions, flags urgent ones, and builds a digest for the CEO to review on the move.

11:00 AM. Vendor contracts need reviewing. Instead of leafing through PDFs, the assistant uploads them to an AI contract analyzer (e.g., Lexion, Ironclad). The system highlights renewal dates, penalty clauses, pricing shifts, and areas flagged for compliance risk. The assistant forwards key points to legal and marks contracts for the CEO's approval queue.

12:00 PM. Lunchtime, but not downtime. The assistant checks real-time hospital metrics via an AI-driven dashboard—bed occupancy, ED wait times, staff shortages. The tool flags when targets aren't met and suggests action items. This is not just data—it's synthesized direction, saving a post-lunch catch-up meeting.

1:00 PM. Afternoon meeting prep. The assistant uses a speech-to-text AI to summarize voice memos left by the CEO and department heads. Action items are tagged, scheduled, and synced with project management software. What once meant frantic note-taking and double data entry is now a seamless flow.

2:30 PM. Patient complaint or incident. The assistant receives a flagged report from the hospital's feedback AI, which clusters related incidents, provides suggested template responses, and alerts the PR lead if escalation is needed. The assistant drafts and dispatches necessary responses without hunting for forms or email threads.

3:30 PM. Physician onboarding requires credential verification and document assembly. The assistant uses AI credentialing tools to auto-collect licensure, references, background checks, and policy acknowledgments. The platform flags missing elements, requests them automatically, and builds a digital folder for HR.

4:30 PM. Final email and task review. The AI triage tool updates the to-do list, surfaces deadlines, and identifies incomplete tasks. The assistant closes the day with a handoff to the night team, generated by the system and customized with personal notes.

By 5:00 PM, what used to be a twelve-hour day finishes in nine. The assistant isn't running less—it's that the "running" is strategic, not reactive.

AI hasn't replaced the job. It's reshaped the flow, moving information forward, reducing dead time, and letting the assistant focus on judgment, relationships, and priorities.

That's how time compounds for the CEO's right hand: not by skipping steps, but by making every step sharper.

32

SOFTWARE SALES DEVELOPMENT REP

8:00 AM. The SDR starts by reviewing the day's outreach plan. Instead of building call lists from scratch, she uses Apollo.io or ZoomInfo's AI-driven lead scoring. The tools automatically rank prospects based on recent activity, job changes, and company funding news. In minutes, she has a prioritized list of high-probability leads to contact first.

8:30 AM. Email outreach. The SDR opens ChatGPT or GrammarlyGO, pastes prospect names, and prompts for personalized cold emails. Each message is customized with the recipient's company, pain points, and recent news (all gathered from LinkedIn and Google News). Rather than sending a hundred copy-paste blasts, she gets twenty high-quality, high-relevance emails out in less than thirty minutes.

9:30 AM. LinkedIn follow-ups. With the help of Taplio or ChatGPT's browser plugin, the SDR generates short, tailored LinkedIn connection requests and follow-up messages. AI summarizes the prospect's activity and suggests questions or value props. The result: more replies, less generic chatter, and less manual browsing.

10:30 AM. Voicemail and call notes. After a round of calls, the SDR uses Otter.ai or Fireflies.ai to transcribe voicemails and summarize key points from each conversation. She pastes these summaries directly into the CRM, skipping the old ritual of manual note-typing.

11:30 AM. Pipeline review. Instead of poring over CRM dashboards and spreadsheets, she asks ChatGPT (or Salesforce Einstein, if available) to summarize pipeline health. The AI highlights at-risk deals, flags follow-up opportunities, and points out gaps in territory coverage. She can act on recommendations instead of just reading static numbers.

12:30 PM. Lunch break and training. The SDR spends fifteen minutes on AI-powered sales training platforms (like Second Nature or Spekit). The system delivers custom micro-modules based on her performance data —objection handling, new product updates, or competitive insights. It's learning, but only what's relevant now.

1:00 PM. Objection handling. On a call, a prospect raises a technical concern about software integrations. The SDR enters the question into ChatGPT, which returns a concise, jargon-free explanation pulled from company docs and public knowledge bases. She shares the answer live, keeping the conversation moving.

2:00 PM. Meeting scheduling. The SDR uses Calendly or Motion, which offer AI scheduling features to find open slots, handle time zones, and even reschedule last minute. She sends links, and meetings land on both calendars instantly—no email ping-pong.

2:30 PM. Demo prep. For prospects ready to see the product, the SDR uses an AI-powered video editing tool (like Descript or Loom's auto-captioning) to create and personalize demo walkthroughs. Each video can be tailored to industry, use case, or even the prospect's logo in the intro. The SDR never waits for marketing; she delivers fast.

3:30 PM. Call recap. After a major sales call, the SDR records a summary into Otter.ai or the phone's voice recorder. ChatGPT or Notion AI converts the transcript into a to-do list, sends follow-up emails, and updates CRM tasks. No backtracking, no missed action items.

4:00 PM. Social listening and competitive tracking. The SDR uses an AI browser extension (like Feedly AI or Perplexity) to monitor for news about prospects, new product launches, or competitor moves. The tool summarizes trends, which the SDR references in her next outreach.

4:30 PM. End-of-day reporting. The SDR uses ChatGPT to draft a concise update for her manager, including stats, highlights, and tomorrow's focus. Instead of scrambling for numbers, she copies summaries directly from the day's activity log.

The result? More targeted outreach, faster responses, and less admin grind. Every step that once dragged is now a quick, AI-accelerated loop.

She isn't making more calls. She's just making better use of every hour—and it shows.

33

NEUROLOGY RESEARCHER

6:30 AM. The researcher arrives early. Before entering the lab, she checks overnight video feeds of the primate housing area. Using an AI-based behavior analysis tool (like DeepLabCut or EthoVision XT), the system flags unusual movement, signs of agitation, or possible health issues. The researcher reviews a condensed highlights reel instead of hours of footage. Early alerts help her prioritize morning welfare checks.

7:00 AM. Animal health review. Digital records are managed with an electronic lab notebook integrated with AI summarization (eLabFTW, Benchling). The AI highlights recent medication changes, feeding deviations, and vet notes. Any flagged changes trigger a prompt check, saving the researcher from hunting through logbooks.

7:30 AM. Protocol prep. The day's experiments require a batch of custom behavioral tasks. The researcher uses ChatGPT or a similar LLM to draft trial scripts for the touchscreen apparatus, then has the AI check them for logical errors and regulatory compliance language. The protocols are saved, versioned, and sent to the Institutional Animal Care and Use Committee (IACUC) for any necessary updates, all in under an hour.

8:30 AM. Team briefing. Voice notes are recorded on Otter.ai during the morning huddle. The app transcribes instructions, schedules, and hazard reminders, auto-sending notes to staff and generating a to-do list for the group. Questions about task assignments or compliance are clarified without delay.

9:00 AM. Experiment setup. The AI-powered tracking system is calibrated for each monkey. These platforms can now identify subtle changes in movement or task performance that might signal neurological changes. The researcher uses a web dashboard that compiles real-time data—no more waiting for post-session video analysis.

10:00 AM. Data collection. As monkeys perform tasks, all touchscreen events and physiological recordings are logged. AI modules (TensorFlow-based custom scripts or commercial tools) flag outlier responses and suggest possible artifacts for review. The researcher sees preliminary trends before the first run ends, not days later.

12:00 PM. Lunch break—paperwork automation. The researcher uses ChatGPT to summarize results, draft progress emails to collaborators, and format citations for a grant report. Reference management is handled by Zotero with AI plug-ins for automatic bibliography updates. Instead of copying and pasting between Word and Excel, she sends the whole report in one sitting.

1:00 PM. Afternoon welfare rounds. The researcher speaks notes into her phone, which Otter.ai transcribes and files directly to the animal's digital record. If the system flags a possible welfare concern, an alert is sent to the facility vet, and a log entry is generated for compliance audits.

2:00 PM. Data analysis. AI-powered statistics software (JASP, GraphPad Prism with scripting) generates graphs and initial models. For complex neural data, the researcher runs dimensionality reduction in Python, prompting ChatGPT for code optimization and troubleshooting. Patterns in firing rates or response times are visualized immediately, accelerating review.

3:30 PM. Grant writing. The researcher uses ChatGPT to draft text for new funding proposals, tailoring responses for NIH guidelines or foundation calls. The AI suggests recent papers and flags missing citations, reducing the research and drafting process from days to hours.

4:30 PM. Compliance review. All logs, video summaries, and daily reports are compiled into an AI-generated regulatory compliance pack, formatted to IACUC standards. Instead of end-of-month panic, the researcher reviews, annotates, and submits the report on time.

5:00 PM. End-of-day summary. The day's activities, animal health notes, and preliminary findings are bundled into an AI-generated digest and sent to the PI and collaborators. Tomorrow's action items are flagged, and the lab is set to run leaner and faster the next day.

AI hasn't made neurology research easy. But it's turned every manual delay—data entry, monitoring, compliance—into a process that runs in the background, letting the science move forward.

34

SOFTWARE ENGINEER

8:30 AM. The engineer begins with a review of overnight code changes. GitHub Copilot or Codeium provides AI-powered code summaries, highlighting pull requests that might require special attention. Instead of reading dozens of diffs line by line, she sees a prioritized list of "most likely to break" and "needs review" items. She triages issues in minutes, not an hour.

9:00 AM. Daily stand-up. Instead of scrambling to recall yesterday's work, she opens Otter.ai, which has transcribed the previous day's meeting and summarized action items. She copies the highlights into the project Slack, making updates visible before anyone asks.

9:30 AM. Ticket planning. The team uses Linear or Jira, but now with AI plugins (Linear's built-in AI or Jira's

Atlassian Intelligence) that auto-suggest priorities based on deadlines, code dependencies, and recent bug reports. She sees which features are likely to block others, and reorders her sprint plan with a few clicks.

10:00 AM. Coding session. As she works, GitHub Copilot autocompletes boilerplate, suggests function names, and even writes whole test files from docstrings. If she gets stuck, she asks ChatGPT for a quick code example, optimization tip, or regex fix. The pace isn't superhuman, but the friction drops out of routine work.

11:30 AM. Code review. Pull requests from teammates arrive. Copilot and ChatGPT offer AI-generated review comments, pointing out edge cases or non-idiomatic code. She makes focused edits, knowing she can rely on a second, tireless "pair programmer" to spot missed details.

12:30 PM. Lunch break—no downtime. She asks ChatGPT to summarize a new API doc or RFC she's been meaning to read. It distills twenty pages into a two-minute abstract, highlighting changes relevant to her stack. She digests the essentials while finishing lunch.

1:00 PM. Debugging. A bug report comes in with an odd stack trace. She pastes it into ChatGPT, which explains the likely root cause, suggests diagnostic steps, and recommends fixes based on community Q&A. Instead of blind trial and error, she has a plan before the next commit.

2:00 PM. Documentation. Instead of manually updating every README, she uses Mintlify or GitBook with AI-powered doc generation. The tools auto-extract docstrings and usage examples, creating up-to-date guides with one command. She reviews and tweaks, but starts at 90% complete.

2:45 PM. Meeting with product. She records the Zoom call and uploads the audio to Otter.ai, which transcribes and summarizes requirements. ChatGPT generates a bullet-point project brief and links open questions to the correct tickets. Context loss between meetings and code drops to zero.

3:30 PM. Refactoring. She selects legacy code for a rewrite. Copilot suggests migration strategies, and ChatGPT provides sample code for new frameworks. Instead of endless Google searches, she moves through the rewrite with clarity.

4:30 PM. End-of-day wrap. The engineer uses a personal Notion or Obsidian database with built-in AI plugins to generate a summary of today's commits, blockers, and tomorrow's plan. The summary is shared with the team, and a to-do list is auto-generated.

By 5:00 PM, every time-sink—code reviews, bug hunts, documentation, even meeting management—has shifted from manual to machine-augmented. The engineer isn't working fewer hours, but every hour is tighter, and every feedback loop is shorter.

AI hasn't changed what it means to build software. It's changed how much time is left for the parts that matter.

35

SMALL BOOK PUBLISHER CEO

7:00 AM. The CEO starts with a review of overnight submissions. Instead of slogging through a crowded inbox, she runs manuscripts and query letters through ChatGPT or Claude to produce quick synopses and red-flag any obvious genre mismatches or problematic content. She skims summaries, flags strong prospects, and deletes obvious misfits—forty minutes of work compressed into fifteen.

8:00 AM. Sales numbers. Using a spreadsheet linked to BookScan, Amazon KDP, and IngramSpark, the CEO triggers an AI dashboard (ChatGPT Advanced Data Analysis or Google Sheets with Gemini) that summarizes sales by title, author, channel, and trend. The report includes recommendations: which books need a price promo, which are showing seasonal spikes, and which backlist titles are quietly accelerating. Decisions land before coffee cools.

9:00 AM. Author communication. ChatGPT drafts individualized emails to authors: royalty statements, marketing updates, cover feedback, or gentle reminders about deadlines. Instead of generic BCCs or endless cutting and pasting, the CEO customizes three to five messages in a few minutes. Every author feels like the only client.

10:00 AM. Editorial meeting. The team uses Otter.ai to transcribe discussions and summarize acquisition decisions, production timelines, and new launch plans. Action items are auto-synced to Asana, where Gemini AI suggests optimal schedules based on dependencies —cover design, proofing, advance reader copy prep, and print deadlines. Bottlenecks are flagged before they can slip.

11:00 AM. Manuscript review. A promising title gets a deeper pass. The CEO prompts ChatGPT to check for internal consistency, pacing issues, or repetition. She asks for a chapter-level outline and a short report on character arcs and thematic threads. This doesn't replace editorial judgment. It accelerates the sift, focusing her attention on creative choices.

12:00 PM. Cover design. The CEO uploads notes to Canva's Magic Design or Midjourney (for early concepting), generating multiple cover mockups in minutes. The AI suggests color palettes and typefaces based on genre, current trends, and comp titles. She selects two directions to send to the designer, who spends time refining, not starting from zero.

1:00 PM. Lunch break. The CEO catches up on industry news, but doesn't scroll endlessly. She asks Perplexity or ChatGPT to summarize the top five trends in publishing, new platform policies, or notable deals in her segment. Highlights are shared with her staff for discussion at the next meeting.

2:00 PM. Metadata and SEO. The CEO feeds back cover blurbs, keywords, and BISAC codes to ChatGPT or Publisher Rocket, ensuring every book's metadata is optimized for Amazon and library discoverability. Suggested tweaks are copied directly to the distributor's dashboard—no more missed categories or bad keywords.

3:00 PM. Marketing content. AI tools draft newsletter copy, ad headlines, and press releases. Canva's Magic Write suggests post topics and hashtags for social campaigns. The CEO reviews, edits, and schedules campaigns across platforms—saving hours on content calendars and design tweaks.

4:00 PM. Contract review. Legal language and new royalty proposals are pasted into ChatGPT for plain-language explanations. The CEO catches problematic clauses before passing the contract to her attorney, reducing time spent in legal back-and-forth.

5:00 PM. End-of-day wrap. The CEO dictates a quick summary of wins, open issues, and tomorrow's top tasks to Otter.ai, which transcribes and emails her action plan. All major loops—submissions, sales, editorial, production, marketing—are closed or handed off for follow-up.

AI hasn't made publishing easy. But it's made the administrative drag manageable, giving the CEO space for judgment, discovery, and the creative risks that build a list.

That's how time compounds at the top of the smallest presses.

36

WRAP UP - HOW AI COMPOUNDS TIME ACROSS JOBS

For the assistant to a hospital CEO, AI-driven triage, scheduling, document drafting, and compliance tools take a ten-hour chaos day and make it a focused eight. Email and calendar friction drop by two-thirds; document prep compresses from hours to minutes. Instead of twelve hours, the assistant routinely finishes in nine, and the day's actual value fits into six. The assistant's energy shifts from triage to strategic problem-solving.

The car salesman, leveraging AI for lead management, customer follow-up, research, and content creation, sees a remarkable shift in daily bandwidth. What once meant eight hours of scattered admin, cold outreach, and note-taking now fits into five hours of targeted work. The salesman's focus moves to high-probability deals, and paperwork, trade appraisals, and follow-ups are condensed from hours to half an hour per task. The eight-hour shift yields the results of a twelve-hour hustle—and less stress.

The sales development rep's time is multiplied at every stage: AI scores leads, drafts emails, summarizes calls, and automates reporting. Hours once spent on research, CRM entry, and follow-up drop to minutes. Outbound outreach that previously took half the day now lands before lunch. The SDR's "real" workload is five focused hours—the rest is discretionary, learning, or pipelining. In effect, AI gives the rep two extra productive days a week.

For the conference manager, every major drag—email, schedule conflicts, vendor updates, reporting—runs in the background. Manual slotting and attendee management are replaced by AI dashboards and chatbots. What was a ten- to twelve-hour day becomes seven. Instead of living in fire-drill mode, the manager operates proactively. Room for actual event management and on-site presence expands, as the invisible admin shrinks.

The neurology researcher finds relief in automated video review, AI health flagging, and rapid data prep. Compliance logs, paperwork, and grant writing compress from days to hours. Each repetitive loop—protocol writing, experiment scripting, data cleaning—is now semi-automated. The effective workday shrinks from ten to six hours, freeing time for deeper analysis and experimental design.

A software engineer, with AI pair programmers, automated documentation, and meeting transcription, sees routine code review, debugging, and doc updates collapse in duration. Morning triage, ticket grooming, and code review loops drop from hours to under an hour each. In practice, an eight-hour engineering day now delivers the output of eleven, with more of it devoted to design and creative problem-solving.

The small book publisher CEO, once buried in admin, now clears submissions, sales reports, author comms, and metadata in record time. Marketing campaigns, contract checks, and cover drafts are handled in minutes, not hours. What was once an endless cycle of interruptions and admin is compressed into four to five high-impact hours. The rest of the day, the CEO is free to scout new titles, strategize, or simply think—a rarity in publishing.

Across these jobs, AI doesn't just "save time." It shifts where time lands—eliminating busywork, surfacing decisions, and leaving each worker with the space to move from reaction to intent. In almost every case, an eight- or ten-hour job is compressed by a third to a half, changing both the tempo and the tone of the work itself.

PART IV

YOU, MULTIPLIED

37

INDIVIDUAL PRODUCTIVITY – COMPRESSING THE PERSONAL WORKFLOW WITH AI

Personal productivity used to hinge on self-discipline, clever hacks, and meticulous lists. What AI brings is structural: the ability to shift hours of prep, research, and admin into background processes. The result isn't just more output—it's output that begins with more clarity and less friction.

The day starts with the inbox. Superhuman and Shortwave both deploy AI-driven email triage, which can summarize, prioritize, and even draft responses. The user no longer sorts through a hundred messages to find what matters. The system highlights key threads and generates reply drafts for routine requests. What took forty minutes becomes a ten-minute review.

Calendar management benefits from x.ai or Reclaim.ai. These tools don't just schedule—they suggest optimal times, block focus periods, and automatically reschedule when meetings overrun. If a last-minute invite comes in, the AI negotiates a time based on everyone's real availability, not endless email ping-pong.

For research, Perplexity.ai is a step change. It synthesizes answers from across the web, pulling sources, summarizing complex topics, and suggesting follow-up questions. Unlike a search engine, it produces a brief you can paste into a memo or project plan. When preparing for meetings, the user inputs agenda topics, and Perplexity produces an actionable summary with references.

Note-taking and knowledge capture shift with Otter.ai and Notion AI. Otter transcribes meetings, interviews, and even voice notes, tagging action items and auto-sharing summaries. Notion AI digests these notes, drafts outlines, and creates follow-up task lists that feed directly into your workflow. The time once spent rewriting or organizing notes now lands in actual project movement.

Content creation—emails, memos, reports, blog posts—compresses further with ChatGPT and Claude. Both models generate, rephrase, or proofread drafts on demand. The user prompts for a 200-word summary, a formal email, or even an executive report, and gets a structured draft in seconds. Editing becomes the main creative work.

Task management grows sharper with Motion, an AI-driven tool that schedules daily tasks, blocks deep work windows, and reprioritizes when something urgent arrives. Unlike static lists, the schedule shifts dynamically, compressing tasks into the most efficient possible sequence.

For social media, Canva's Magic Write and Buffer's AI assistant suggest captions, hashtags, and content ideas. They generate visuals and text posts that fit the user's brand and goals, turning what was an hour's work into ten minutes of quick approvals.

When it comes to learning or upskilling, platforms like Khanmigo (Khan Academy's AI tutor) and Duolingo Max offer real-time feedback, personalized lesson sequencing, and targeted drill sessions. Instead of passive consumption, the user gets interactive, adaptive instruction, learning faster in shorter bursts.

Finally, personal finance and data review are streamlined by tools like Tiller and YNAB, both of which use automation and AI categorization to summarize spending, flag anomalies, and produce reports. Manual spreadsheet entry and monthly reconciliations drop to a few review clicks per week.

Across these tools, the pattern is always the same: time spent on setup, sorting, and status-checking is handed off to the machine. The user focuses on decisions, communication, and output—the things that actually matter.

AI doesn't make anyone superhuman. But it makes the hours between distraction and delivery fewer—and sharper. That's real productivity: not just working more, but wasting less.

38

CALENDAR AS COMMAND CENTER – INTEGRATING SCHEDULING AI TO OFFLOAD PRIORITIZATION

For most professionals, the calendar is a record of what's already lost: back-to-back meetings, cluttered blocks, missed focus time, and a parade of reminders. Productivity advice says to "own your schedule," but the reality is constant triage. AI-driven scheduling finally changes that—not by removing commitments, but by restructuring them around priorities and momentum.

x.ai was one of the first to make AI scheduling feel like a natural extension of the workday. Its AI assistant handled meeting requests, found overlaps, and even negotiated time slots with outside parties. While the original x.ai product is gone, the concept lives on in more robust tools.

Reclaim.ai has taken this further. It auto-blocks focus time, lunch, and personal routines, while integrating task lists and priorities from Google Calendar, Todoist, Asana, and Slack. The AI reviews your commitments, predicts overbookings, and reschedules low-priority tasks around hard deadlines. If a project meeting runs long or a new task is flagged as urgent, the AI reshuffles your entire week in seconds. The effect is subtle but profound: instead of losing hours to reactive rescheduling, you move through your day on rails.

Motion is another tool compressing the chaos. It builds a dynamic daily plan, shuffling tasks and meetings into open slots, and reprioritizes automatically when you fall behind or something new appears. Tasks are dragged from email, Slack, or calendar events. AI figures out where they fit—protecting deep work windows and surfacing critical deadlines. Unlike static to-do lists, your plan is live and adapts as circumstances shift.

For team scheduling, Clockwise uses AI to find common meeting times while preserving everyone's focus blocks. The system scans calendars, flags meeting overload, and proposes "no meeting days" or shared deep work periods. Employees see more white space, and group sessions are sequenced to minimize context switching.

Sunsama blends calendar and task management, using AI to suggest daily priorities based on your goals and past work rhythms. It prompts you to set intentions, import tasks, and evaluate whether you're working in line with your long-term focus. Distractions are minimized, and the week's plan stays anchored in your actual objectives—not just in a sea of requests.

For freelancers or solopreneurs, SavvyCal's AI-powered scheduling links offer a personalized booking experience. The tool scans your open slots, client preferences, and even previous meeting times to suggest the path of least resistance. The client sees only what's really available, and reschedules are handled without manual wrangling.

The real gain is not just saved minutes, but compounded attention. When AI sequences your day, priority tasks land in optimal windows. Interruptions are absorbed with minimal friction, and admin work moves to the margins. Your calendar becomes a command center, not a graveyard of missed intentions.

This shift isn't hypothetical. Anyone with a browser can trial these tools today. Integration takes minutes. The result is a feedback loop: less time spent wrangling the calendar, more time spent in actual work. When your schedule moves at the speed of your goals, every meeting and task is less a block—and more a launchpad.

AI-powered calendar management is not about controlling every minute. It's about moving through the day with structure that responds, rather than resists.

That's what turns a calendar into a command center.

39

INBOX ZERO WITH AUTONOMOUS AGENTS

Email was supposed to be fast. It became a second job—hundreds of messages, scattered requests, and endless threads that drown the signal in noise. The "inbox zero" movement promised a path to sanity, but for most, it required monk-like discipline and daily sacrifices. AI-powered autonomous agents change this equation—not by just filtering, but by actively moving messages forward.

Tools like Shortwave, Superhuman, and Google's new AI-backed Gmail features now do more than highlight important senders. They summarize long threads, extract action items, and cluster related messages, letting you process a day's worth of email in a glance. Shortwave, for instance, reads every thread, groups them by project or urgency, and offers batch archiving for anything you don't need to see. A morning that started with fifty unread emails is triaged to five critical decisions in under fifteen minutes.

Drafting replies has been transformed. ChatGPT and Claude can be connected (often via browser extensions or Zapier workflows) to generate context-aware responses for common requests. Instead of copy-pasting templates or retyping polite "thank yous," users review AI-drafted messages, add personal nuance, and hit send. Even complex, multi-thread negotiations get initial drafts—saving the mental load for final edits.

For customer service or high-traffic inboxes, tools like Front or Hiver route messages to the right teammate, escalate urgent queries, and track response times. The AI learns from your patterns, proposing auto-replies for status updates or meeting invites. Instead of wading through backlog, the user surfaces only what truly requires attention.

Summarization isn't limited to email. SaneBox uses AI to sort newsletters, receipts, and promotions into side folders, ensuring your main inbox remains a work queue, not a junkyard. The time once lost to "checking" is reclaimed for real work. For executives, personal assistants can have access to an AI layer that proposes reply drafts, calendar blocks, or quick summary digests—freeing them for strategic work.

AI agents are also now being built atop open-source tools like Auto-GPT and Taskade, which can parse, categorize, and automate routine inbox tasks. These platforms learn from user correction, meaning every day spent using the system makes it smarter.

The shift is visible at the end of each week. Instead of hundreds of emails responded to in fits and starts, you review and act in two or three focused batches. Outbound messages become sharper, and the cognitive drain of context switching vanishes. For high-velocity environments, the compounding effect is even more dramatic—entire threads move forward while you're in meetings or offline.

Inbox zero is no longer a badge of honor for the obsessively organized. With autonomous agents, it's the natural result of well-sequenced tools that route, summarize, and draft—leaving your time for actual decisions and conversations that matter.

AI doesn't make email go away. It just means you finally get to leave the inbox—and stay out.

40

MEETING ELIMINATION THROUGH AI NOTEBOTS

No more status updates—just transcripts and task syncs.

Meetings consume more time than almost any other part of modern work. Most aren't about decisions—they're about status: what's done, what's stuck, who owns what next. For decades, knowledge workers have lamented the "could have been an email" epidemic. AI notebots are now making that a reality—not by recording meetings, but by making most of them obsolete.

Otter.ai, Fireflies.ai, and Grain are leading the charge. These platforms join Zoom, Teams, or in-person sessions, transcribe everything in real time, and then use AI to summarize the discussion. Crucially, they identify action items, decisions, and open questions.

The result is a post-meeting package delivered to every participant. For routine check-ins or status updates, this summary replaces the need for attendance. If you miss the meeting, you review the digest and move on.

Task sync happens automatically. Otter.ai can now push action items into Asana, Notion, or Trello. Fireflies.ai links tasks to calendar invites and sends follow-up nudges as deadlines approach. Instead of rehashing what was said, everyone works from the same record.

For recurring meetings, AI notebots track progress across weeks. They flag repeated issues, missed deliverables, and shifting priorities, providing a living project memory. Teams spend less time "getting on the same page" and more time advancing actual work.

Even brainstorming is enhanced. Grain and Supernormal let users clip key moments and share highlights, creating asynchronous briefings for leadership or absent team members. Whole departments can now review a major meeting in five minutes instead of an hour-long replay.

More advanced users build workflows with Zapier or Make: when a meeting transcript lands, the AI summarizes it, generates next steps, and emails or slacks the team—zero manual coordination required.

Over time, the result is fewer meetings—because the system proves most are redundant. Updates land in project trackers, roadblocks are flagged by AI, and only sessions that truly require live debate survive. The culture shifts from "default to meeting" to "default to async." Employees find more deep work time and less calendar gridlock.

AI notebots haven't made meetings disappear entirely. But for the first time, the default is clarity and action, not endless rehashing.

41

SECOND BRAIN SYSTEMS

The promise of a "second brain" is more than hype: it's the difference between spending hours searching for a file or insight, and having your past work, notes, and research surface just when you need them. AI is now bringing generative recall to personal knowledge management—making it possible to query years of content as easily as talking to a trusted advisor.

Notion AI is the centerpiece for many. It ingests notes, documents, links, and to-dos, then lets users prompt for summaries, related pages, or synthesis of all notes on a topic. Instead of manual tagging or elaborate hierarchies, the system connects ideas through semantic search and retrieval.

Obsidian with the Smart Connections or Text Generator plugins brings this to local note files. AI suggests links between notes, surfaces recurring themes, and drafts new content that draws from your entire vault. What used to be "out of sight, out of mind" now lives at your fingertips.

For research-heavy roles, tools like Mem.ai and Roam Research (with AI add-ons) build living graphs of information. Users ask, "What did I learn about CRISPR last year?" or "Summarize all my client project retrospectives," and the AI builds an answer, referencing past notes and documents.

Readwise Reader brings in highlights from books, articles, and PDFs, turning scattered marginalia into an interconnected, searchable base. The AI pulls out quotes, creates summaries, and proposes flashcards for learning or review.

Even email and calendar entries can be woven in: tools like Amplecap and Reflect AI sync across platforms, building a holistic personal database that answers questions in seconds.

The real value isn't just search—it's recall at the right moment. Before a client call, the system reminds you of past meeting notes and shared action items. When drafting a proposal, previous templates and lessons-learned land instantly. Creativity compounds because context isn't lost; it's surfaced as needed.

Second brains aren't about hoarding data. They're about offloading memory, letting the mind focus on problem-solving and synthesis. AI turns the archive from static storage to active collaborator—quietly compounding productivity with every new link and retrieval.

42

VOICE-TO-WORK

The voice is the fastest interface most people have, but until recently, it was wasted on reminders, dictation, or voicemails. AI now closes the loop: you speak, and work happens—notes are transcribed, tasks are executed, documents are generated, and apps are triggered, all with minimal lag.

Otter.ai and Whisper (by OpenAI) are top-tier for real-time transcription, offering high-accuracy capture of meetings, phone calls, and even ambient conversation. The system splits speakers, tags action items, and instantly produces a shareable record. The days of "could you repeat that?" are gone.

For direct action, voice command tools like Voiceflow and Speechly let users build custom workflows. You can say, "Send a summary of this meeting to the marketing team," or "Draft an email to the product group outlining next steps," and the AI builds and sends it, no keyboard needed.

On smartphones, Siri Shortcuts and Google Assistant now link voice commands to complex automations: "Schedule a call with Ron," "Add this idea to Notion," or "Summarize my latest emails." When paired with ChatGPT or Taskade, these routines draft text, set reminders, and even update spreadsheets—hands-free.

For content creators, Descript turns spoken narration into edited podcast episodes or explainer videos, editing audio by simply editing the transcript. The workflow moves from real-time speech to final product in a single environment.

Power users chain these tools together: speak a note into Otter, have it transcribed and summarized by ChatGPT, and push action items to Todoist or Asana automatically. Meetings become project plans, brainstorming becomes slides, and spontaneous ideas become organized notes—all by voice.

The result is a workflow that moves at the pace of thought. Typing, copying, and pasting fade into the background. The friction between idea and execution shrinks, and productivity compounds with every word spoken.

Voice-to-work is not just a convenience—it's a shift to working at the speed of your mind, with AI handling the details.

43

VISUAL THINKING VIA AI VIDEO
TOOLS

The whiteboard used to be where ideas took shape—flowcharts, mind maps, and sketches that clarified the next steps. But translating those visuals into explainer videos or shareable presentations was a slow, manual job. AI video tools are now closing that gap, making it possible to move from a rough drawing to a polished animation in a single afternoon.

Tome and Gamma.app lead the charge with AI-powered presentation builders. Users sketch an idea or outline a process, and the tool generates slide decks, visuals, and speaker notes that can be turned into animated explainers. Content is auto-arranged, illustrated, and narrated by AI, producing a final product that looks studio-made.

Runway and Synthesia let creators turn text prompts or whiteboard snapshots into short video segments, complete with avatars or voiceover. You can upload a photo of your hand-drawn diagram, have the system trace and animate the elements, and add AI-generated narration. The result: custom explainer videos for team training, product launches, or classroom instruction.

For educators and trainers, Canva's Magic Design and Animoto simplify storyboard-to-video conversion. You upload screenshots or flowcharts, select a theme, and AI generates transitions, voiceover scripts, and callouts.

Miro and FigJam integrate with generative AI to turn sticky notes and flowcharts into slide decks or story-boards. After a brainstorming session, you ask the AI to "summarize this mind map as a five-slide explainer," and the work is done before the team leaves the room.

AI-driven video tools don't make visual thinking obsolete. They amplify it, compressing the slowest part of ideation—the move from napkin sketch to clear, shared artifact.

In teams where speed matters, the difference is night and day: ideas get tested, refined, and shared in hours, not weeks. Visuals become assets, not bottlenecks.

The real power is not just making videos faster—it's unlocking the ability to think and communicate in images, with AI smoothing every step from sketch to screen.

ADOPTION, FRICTION, AND WHAT COMES NEXT

The promise of compounding time is real, but in practice, the path is rarely smooth. Every tool that compresses hours into minutes also creates a new kind of friction—not technical, but human. Teams, departments, and whole industries are built on the inertia of old routines.

Meetings persist because they are familiar.

Paperwork lingers because it is safe.

Even solo operators, who have the most to gain, will resist automation if it threatens their sense of mastery or control.

That is the adoption curve: it is rarely about access to

new technology, but about willingness to leave behind the rituals that waste time.

Friction comes in several forms. Sometimes it is skepticism—the belief that AI is a toy, a fad, or a risk. Sometimes it is pride. Workers and managers alike can view new tools as threats to their expertise, not as partners in progress. Most often, it is a question of trust.

People want to see proof before they surrender familiar systems, and AI—at least at first—rarely feels "proven" enough to replace muscle memory.

Organizations that break through this resistance share a few traits.

First, they surface wins early and publicly. Small automations, like auto-summarized meetings or inbox triage, are visible and impossible to ignore.

Second, they celebrate time returned as a gain, not as a new burden. If the response to efficiency is simply more busywork, resentment builds.

Clued-in leaders reinforce that compounded time is meant for focus, rest, or bigger swings, not just for filling more boxes. Third, they create templates. One successful workflow becomes a model for another.

Repetition breeds confidence, and confidence dissolves skepticism.

You can do the same. Try compressing just one loop: automate notes, or delegate data cleaning, or script calendar tasks. Notice how quickly it becomes the default.

Adoption is contagious when results are clear and the learning curve is shallow. The mistake is to try to change everything at once. Instead, find the biggest daily friction and let AI handle it for a week. The rest will follow.

The risk, of course, is that compression turns into acceleration. There is a trap where every hour saved becomes another hour filled with new demands. So in effect you could wind up getting paid the same for 5 times as much work.

Efficiency, unmanaged, becomes a new form of overload. That is why the goal is not just more output, but a redesign of where attention lands.

The best use of compounded time is not to work endlessly, but to think deeper, solve harder problems, or step back from the grind.

Looking ahead, the curve is only going to steepen. LLMs and AI agents will soon move from supporting roles to active team members. They will monitor projects, propose changes, and flag bottlenecks before humans notice them. Teams will look less like static charts and more like shifting collaborations of people, tools, and models.

The gap between organizations that embrace time compounding and those that wait will widen, and the winners will not be the ones who automate first, but the ones who make compounding part of their operating rhythm.

I don't think this future is about being the fastest adopter. It is about being the most, and I really hate this word, "intentional." Adoption is not a switch; it is a habit. Friction is not an enemy; it is a signal that something is ready to be improved.

A good strategy is to approach every process as a candidate for compression, knowing that the real value of AI is not in the code, but in the time and clarity it returns.

The world is going to get faster, but not necessarily better. Whether you win or lose in this new landscape will depend on your ability to spot friction, adopt the right changes, and invest your reclaimed hours where they matter most.

Compounding time is a competitive advantage, but only for those willing to lean into change, manage the pace, and use every new minute wisely.

That is the real frontier; one that is open to anyone, but claimed by those who move first and move smart.

BIBLIOGRAPHY

I did a lot of reading while I was thinking this book through. And here are the books that helped me the most preparing to get this project done. I'm not going to tell you to read all of them.

But you probably should.

- **Competing Against Time** by George Stalk Jr. & Thomas Hout. The original treatise on time as competitive advantage, focusing on sequence, flow, and velocity in business.
- **Making Space: How the Brain Knows Where Things Are** by Jennifer M. Groh. A groundbreaking exploration of the neuroscience behind spatial awareness, mapping how the brain locates, tracks, and remembers objects in the world—a must-read for understanding how attention, perception, and action are woven together in daily life.
- **The Goal: A Process of Ongoing Improvement** by Eliyahu M. Goldratt. A foundational systems-thinking book on bottlenecks and operational flow, written as a business novel.
- **Deep Work: Rules for Focused Success in a Distracted World** by Cal Newport. Goes beyond "focus" to show how structure and sequence compound results in knowledge work.
- **Artificial Intelligence: A Modern Approach** by Stuart Russell & Peter Norvig. The definitive textbook on AI, combining foundational theory with real-world applications. Covers search, reasoning, learning, language,

vision, and ethics—an indispensable reference for understanding both how AI works and where it's heading.

- **Four Thousand Weeks: Time Management for Mortals** by Oliver Burkeman. A philosophical, contrarian book about the limits of optimization and the real meaning of time.

- **Making Work Visible: Exposing Time Theft to Optimize Work & Flow** by Dominica DeGrandis. An actionable guide to finding bottlenecks, invisible work, and time waste in teams and organizations.

- **The Checklist Manifesto: How to Get Things Right** by Atul Gawande. Shows how checklists reduce friction, error, and delay—critical for compressing time in complex work.

- **Slack: Getting Past Burnout, Busywork, and the Myth of Total Efficiency** by Tom DeMarco. Explores why slack is strategic in systems, and how "always-on" efficiency can backfire.

- **How to Take Smart Notes: One Simple Technique to Boost Writing, Learning and Thinking** by Sönke Ahrens. Introduces the Zettelkasten method—a structured approach to linked personal knowledge.

- **Seeing Like a State: How Certain Schemes to Improve the Human Condition Have Failed** by James C. Scott. A systems-level critique of legibility, control, and the hidden risks in large-scale redesign.

TOOLS I USED TO WRITE THIS BOOK

Writing a book about compounding time means practicing what you preach. Every tool I used for this project was chosen for one reason: it reduced friction. The tech stack is not futuristic. It is practical, reliable, and relentlessly focused on workflow.

DevonThink was my external brain. It organized research, archived web pages, and allowed me to retrieve quotes and references in seconds. Nothing gets lost, nothing gets duplicated. If you care about searchable knowledge, DevonThink is where you store it.

Apple Pages handled final text clean-up and formatting. It is fast, stable, and plays well with everything else on the Mac. When the time came for a readable, clean export, Pages delivered.

BBEdit took care of batch editing, regex-driven search and replace, and text transformations. If you want control over raw text, nothing is faster.

Vellum is what made the book a book. It handled print and eBook layout with minimal fuss. Styles, previews, and output for multiple platforms—all rendered exactly as promised. It is the closest thing to publishing without a learning curve.

Keyboard Maestro provided the automation glue. From repetitive window management to boilerplate insertion, it turned five-step routines into a single keystroke. Every little automation helped.

Emacs org-mode (yes, the "superpower" mentioned in the book) kept notes, todos, and drafts organized in plain text. Hierarchical outlining, code snippets, and date-stamped notes—all in one buffer.

ChatGPT was the accelerator. It provided summaries, rewrites, new angles, and more than once the blunt prompt that got me past a stuck paragraph. OF COURSE it helped me write. Just look for the paragraphs with the em-dash. Dead giveaway.

The point is not the brand or the software. The point is sequence. Each tool did its job. Each one cut friction. The sum was more than the parts. If you want to write faster, think clearer, or just work with less drag, your stack matters. These are the tools that worked for me.

Ron Galloway

You, Multiplied (v1.0 June 2025)

ABOUT THE AUTHOR

I am Ron Galloway. I have been a researcher for 38 years. I am the author of several books on technology in the "Clear & To The Point™" series, and I have made 4 films. I have keynoted 600+ conferences.

I'm a graduate of Georgia Tech. I was an analyst at Robinson-Humphrey/American Express, then Smith Barney, then spent 10 years at an analytical RIA. In 2006 I started a research company, and have been happily reading since.

Odds & Ends: My documentary on WalMart was the first film ever to premiere in the US Capitol Building. That was random. For some reason I made a film on the neuroscience of PowerPoint.

I speak at conferences and board meetings quite frequently. If you're interested in having me speak, please visit www.rongalloway.com

𝕏 x.com/rongalloway

ABOUT THE SERIES

The *Clear & To The Point* series was created for professionals, thinkers, and builders who want clarity, not clutter.

Each book is built on the principle that complexity can be explained without condescension, and that the best ideas need fewer words, not more.

We cut through jargon, abstractions, and management-speak to get to the real mechanisms that drive results.

Whether the subject is technology, health, strategy, or workflow, the focus is always the same: what works, why it matters, and how to use it.

Our goal is simple. Deliver insight that's operational, actionable, and built for people who are already busy.

Every volume in the series is well-researched, field-tested, and designed for professionals who need answers, not theory. If you want hype, there are plenty of other places to find it. If you want books that make sense on the first read, and hold up on the second, this series was built for you.

You can find the *Clear & To The Point* Series everywhere you order books online.

Visit us at www.clearandtothepoint.com

ALSO BY RON GALLOWAY

BOOKS: CLEAR & TO THE POINT SERIES

AI: Clear & To The Point

Tech Terms For Trustees

Sector Zero

Data To Dignosis

FILMS

Why WalMart Works

Rethinking Powerpoint

Black Box Doc

FWMD: Financial Weapons Of Mass Distruction

www.ingramcontent.com/pod-product-compliance
Lightning Source LLC
Chambersburg PA
CBHW040919210326
41597CB00030B/5125

* 9 7 8 1 9 2 8 8 8 5 7 6 4 *